Thomas More, Gilbert Burnet

Utopia or The Happy Republic

A Philosophical Romance

Thomas More, Gilbert Burnet

Utopia or The Happy Republic
A Philosophical Romance

ISBN/EAN: 9783743422162

Manufactured in Europe, USA, Canada, Australia, Japa

Cover: Foto ©Thomas Meinert / pixelio.de

Manufactured and distributed by brebook publishing software (www.brebook.com)

Thomas More, Gilbert Burnet

Utopia or The Happy Republic

UTOPIA:

OR THE
HAPPY REPUBLIC;

A

PHILOSOPHICAL ROMANCE,

IN TWO BOOKS.

BOOK I. Containing preliminary difcourfes on the happieft ftate of a common-wealth.	The towns, magiftrates, mechanic trades, and manner of life of the Utopians,
BOOK II. Containing a defcription of the ifland of Utopia,	Their traffic, travelling, flaves, marriages, military difcipline, religions.

WRITTEN IN LATIN
BY SIR THOMAS MORE,
Lord High Chancellor of England.

TRANSLATED INTO ENGLISH
BY GILBERT BURNET D. D.
Sometime Profeffor of Divinity in the Univerfity of Glafgow,
afterwards Bifhop of Sarum.

GLASGOW:
PRINTED BY ROBERT AND ANDREW FOULIS,
M.DCC.LXII.

BISHOP BURNET'S
PREFACE
CONCERNING
TRANSLATION,
PARTICULARLY THIS OF
UTOPIA.

THERE is no way of writing so proper, for the refining and polishing a language, as the translating of books into it, if he that undertakes it has a competent skill of the one tongue, and is a master of the other. When a man writes his own thoughts, the heat of his fancy, and the quickness of his mind, carry him so much after the notions themselves, that for the most part he is too warm to judge of the aptness of words, and the justness of figures; so that he either neglects these too much, or over-does them: but when a man translates, he has none of these heats about him: and therefore the French took no ill method, when they intended to reform and beautify their language, in setting their best writers on work to translate the Greek and Latin authors into it. There is so little praise got by translations, that a man cannot be engaged to it out of vanity, for it has passed for a sign of a slow mind, that can amuse itself with so mean an entertainment; but we begin to grow wiser, and tho' ordinary translators must succeed ill in the esteem of the world, yet some have appeared of late that will, I hope, bring that way of writing in credit. The English language has wrought itself out, both of the fulsome pedantry under which it laboured long ago, and the trifling way of dark and unintelligible wit that came after that, and out of the coarse extravagance of canting that succeeded this: but as one extream commonly produces another, so we were beginning to fly into a sublime pitch of a strong but false rhetoric, which had much corrupted, not only the stage, but even the pulpit; two places, that tho' they ought not to be named together, much less to resemble one another; yet it cannot be denied, but the rule and measure of speech is generally taken from them: but that florid strain is almost quite worn out, and is become now as ridiculous as it was once admired. So that without either the expence or labour that the French have undergone, our language has, like a rich wine, wrought out its tartar, and is insensibly brought to a purity that could not have been compassed without much labour, had it not been for the great advantage that we have of a prince, who is so great a judge, that his single approbation or dislike has almost as great an authority over our language, as his prerogative gives him over our coin. We are now so much refined, that how de-

THE PREFACE.

fective soever our imaginations or reasonings may be, yet our language has fewer faults, and is more natural and proper, than it was ever at any time before. When one compares the best writers of the last age, with those that excel in this, the difference is very discernible: even the great Sir Francis Bacon, that was the first that writ our language correctly; as he is still our best author, yet in some places has figures so strong, that they could not pass now before a severe judge. I will not provoke the present masters of the stage, by preferring the authors of the last age to them: for tho' they all acknowledge that they come far short of B. Johnson, Beaumont and Fletcher, yet I believe they are better pleased to say this themselves, than to have it observed by others. Their language is now certainly properer, and more natural than it was formerly, chiefly since the correction that was given by the Rehearsal; and it is to be hop'd, that the essay on poetry, which may be well matched with the best pieces of its kind that even Augustus's age produced, will have a more powerful operation, if clear sense, joined with home but gentle reproofs, can work more on our writers, than that unmerciful exposing of them has done.

I have now much leisure, and want diversion, so I have bestowed some of my hours upon translations, in which I have proposed no ill patterns to myself: but the reader will be best able to judge whether I have copied skilfully after such originals. This small volume which

THE PREFACE.

I now publish, being writ by one of the greatest men that this island has produced, seemed to me to contain so many fine and well digested notions, that I thought it might be no unkind nor ill entertainment to the nation, to put a book in their hands, to which they have so good a title, and which has a very common fate upon it, to be more known and admired all the world over, than here at home. It was once translated into English not long after it was written; and I was once apt to think it might have been done by Sir Thomas More himself: for as it is in the English of his age, and not unlike his style; so the translator has taken a liberty that seems too great for any but the author himself, who is master of his own book, and so may leave out or alter his original as he pleases: which is more than a translator ought to do, I am sure it is more than I have presumed to do.

It was writ in the year 1516, as appears by the date of the letter of Peter Gile's, in which he says, that it was sent him but a few days before from the author, and that bears date the first of November that year; but I cannot imagine how he comes to be called sheriff of London in the title of the book, for in all our printed catalogues of sheriffs, his name is not to be found. I do not think myself concerned in the matter of his book, no more than any other translator is in his author: nor do I think More himself went in heartily to that which is the chief basis of his Utopia, the taking away of all property, and the levelling the world; but that he only intended to set many notions in his reader's way; and that he might not seem too much in earnest, he went so far out of all roads to do it the less suspected: the earnestness with which he recommends the precaution used in marriages among the Utopians, makes one think that he had a misfortune in his own choice, and that therefore he was so cautious on that head; for the strictness of his life covers him from severe censures: his setting out so barbarous a practice, as the hiring of assassines to take off enemies is so wild and so immoral both, that it does not admit of any thing to soften or excuse it, much less to justify it; and the advising men in some cases to put an end to their lives, notwithstanding all the caution with which he guards it, is a piece of rough and fierce philosophy. The tenderest part of the whole work, was the representation he gives of Henry the seventh's court; and his discourses upon it, towards the end of the first book, in which his disguise is so thin, that the matter would not have been much plainer if he had named him: but when he ventured to write so freely of the father in the son's reign, and to give such an idea of government under the haughtiest prince, and the most impatient of uneasy restraints that ever reigned in England, who yet was so far from being displeased with him for it, that as he made him long his particular friend, so he employed him in all his affairs afterwards, and raised him to be Lord Chancellor, I thought I

THE PREFACE.

might venture to put it in more modern Englifh: for as the tranflators of Plutarch's Hero's, or of Tully's Offices, are not concerned, either in the maxims, or in the actions that they relate; fo I, who only tell, in the beft Englifh I can, what Sir Thomas More writ in very elegant Latin, muft leave his thoughts and notions to the reader's cenfure, and do think myfelf liable for nothing but the fidelity of the tranflation, and the correctnefs of the Englifh; and for that I can only fay, that I have writ as carefully, and as well as I can.

TESTIMONIES
CONCERNING
SIR THOMAS MORE,

By Great and Learned men of different Nations and Religions.

Extracted from the History of his LIFE, written by his Great-grand-son. printed at London 1627.

CARDINAL POOL.

STRANGERS and men of other nations, that never had seen him in their lives, received so much grief at the hearing of his death, reading the story thereof, they could not refrain from weeping, bewailing an unknown person only famous unto them for his worthy acts: yea, I cannot hold myself from weeping as I write, tho' I be far off my country; I loved him dearly, who had not so many urgent causes of his love, as many others had, only in respect of his virtues and heroical acts, for which he was a most necessary member of his country; and now God is my witness, I shed for him, even whether I would or no, so many tears, that they hinder me from writing, and often blot out the letters quite, which I am framing, that I can proceed no farther.—Thy father, oh London! thy ornament, thy defence, was brought to his death, being innocent in thy sight; by birth, thy child; by condition, thy citizen, but thy father for the many benefits done unto thee; for he shewed more evident signs of his fatherly love towards thee, than ever any loving father hath expressed to his only and truly beloved child; yet in nothing hath he more declared his fatherly affection, than by his end; for that he lost his life for thy sake.—Wherefore that which we read in the ancient stories of Greece, as touching Socrates, whom the Athenians condemned most unjustly to take poison, so thou hast now seen thy Socrates beheaded before thine eyes; a while after his death, when in a play there was recited out of a tragedy these words: 'You have slain, you have slain 'the best man of all Greece.' Upon these their words every man so lamented the death of Socrates, calling to mind that injustice, altho' the poet himself dreamed least of him, that the whole theater was filled with nothing else, but tears and howling, for which cause the people presently revenged his death, by punishing grievously the chief authors thereof; those that were of them to be found, were put to death presently, and they that could not be found out, were banished. There was also a statue erected in his honour, in the very market-place. If they therefore at the only hearing of these words upon the stage took an occasion to be revenged of that most innocent man's slaughter; what more just cause may'st thou, London, have of compassion and revenge, hearing the like words to these, not pronounced only by any stage-player at home, but by most grave and reverend men in all places of christendom, when as they speak most seriously, exprobrating often unto thee thine ingratitude, and saying: 'You have slain, you have 'slain the best English-man alive.

ERASMUS.

EVERY man bewaileth the death of Sir THOMAS MORE, even they who are adversaries unto him for religion; so great was his courtesie to all men, so great his affability, so excellent was his nature. Whom did he ever send away from him, if he were any thing learned, without gifts? Or who was so great a stranger unto him, to whom he did not seek to do one good turn or other? Many are favourable only to their own countrymen; Frenchmen to Frenchmen, Germans to Germans, Scottishmen to Scots. But the friendship of his generous soul extended to Irish, to French, to Germans, to Scots. This his bounty hath so engraven MORE in every man's heart, that they all lament his death, as the loss of their own father or brother; I myself have seen many tears come from those men who never saw MORE in their lives, nor ever received any benefit from him; yea, whilst I writ these things, tears gush from me whether I will or no. How many souls hath that axe wounded, which cut of MORE's head?

JO. COCHLEUS.

WHAT praise or honour could you get by that cruelty, which you exercised against Sir THOMAS MORE? He was a man of most known and laudable humanity, mild behaviour, affability, bounty, eloquence, wisdom, innocency of life, wit, learning, exceedingly beloved and admired of all men; in dignity, besides, highest judge of your country, and next to the king himself, famous from his youth; beneficial to his country for many embassages, and now most venerable for his gray head, drawing towards old age, who having obtained of the king an honourable dismission from his office, lived privately at home with his wife, children, and nephews, having never committed the least offence against any, burdensome to no man, ready to help every body, mild and pleasant of disposition. You have given counsel to have this so good a man drawn out of his own house, out of that sweet academy of learned and devout Christian Philosophers, for no other cause but this, that he would not justify your impieties; his guiltless conscience resisting it, the fear of God, and his soul's health withdrawing him from it. Do you believe that this your wicked fact hath ever pleased any one of what nation, sex, or age soever?

PAULUS JOVIUS.

FORTUNE, fickle and unconstant, after her accustomed manner, and always hating virtue, if ever she play'd the part of a proud and cruel dame, she hath lately behaved herself most cruelly in England, under Henry the eight, casting down before her Thomas More, whom the king, whilst he was an excellent admirer of virtue, had raised to the highest places of honour in his realm, that from thence, being by fatal madness changed into a beast, he might suddenly throw him down again with great cruelty, because he would not favour the unsatiable lust of that furious tyrant, and for that he would not flatter him in his wickedness, being a man most eminent for the accomplishment of all parts of justice, and most saintly in all kinds of virtues. For when the king would be divorced from his lawful wife, marry a queen, and hasten to disinherit, with shame, his lawful daughter (Mary,) MORE Lord Chancellor was forced to appear at the bar guilty only for his piety and innocency, and there was condemned most wrongfully to a most cruel and shameful death like a traitor and murderer, so that it was not lawful for his friends to bury the dismembred quarters of his body. But Henry for this fact, an imitator of Phalaris, shall never be able to bereave him of perpetual fame, by this his unlawful wickedness, but that the name of MORE shall remain constant and in honour, by his famous Utopia.

JO. RIVIUS, a learned PROTESTANT.

HE that is in a prince's court, ought freely, if he be asked his judgment, rather to tell his mind plainly, what is most behoofeful for his prince's good, than to speak placentia, tickling his ears with flattery; neither ought he to praise things which are not praise-worthy, nor to dispraise maters that are worthy of high commendations; yea, altho' he be in danger of getting no favour by persuading it, but rather punishment and disgrace for gainsaying men's appetites.——Such a man was lately in our memory that singular and excellent for learning and piety, yea, the only ornament and glory of his country THOMAS MORE, who because he would not agree to nor approve by his consent, against his own conscience, the new marriage of the king of England, who would needs be divorced from his first wife, and marry another, he was first cast into prison, one that had singularly well-deserved of the king himself, and of England; and when he constantly continued in his opinion, which he truly thought to be most just, most lawful and godly, emboldened to defend it by a sincere conscience, he was put to death, by that wicked parricide, that most hateful and cruel tyrant; a cruelty not heard of before in this our age. Oh ingratitude and singular impiety of the king's, who could first endure to consume and macerate with a tedious and loathsome imprisonment, such a sincere and holy good man; one that had been so careful of his glory, so studious of his country's profit; he that had persuaded him always to all justice and honesty, dissuaded him from all contraries, and not convinced of any crime, nor found in any fault, he slew him (Oh miserable wickedness!) not only being innocent, but him that had deserved high rewards, and his most faithful and trusty councellor. Are these thy rewards, O king? is this the thanks thou returnest him for all his trusty service and good-will unto thee? Doth this man reap this commodity for his moſt faithful acts and employ-ments? But, oh MORE, thou art now happy, and enjoyeſt eternal felicity, who wouldſt loſe thy head rather than approve any thing againſt thine own conſcience, who more eſteemeſt righteouſneſs, juſtice and piety, than life itſelf; and whilſt thou art deprived of this mortal life, thou paſſeſt to the true and immortal happineſs of heaven; whilſt thou are taken away from men, thou art raiſed up amongſt the numbers of holy ſaints and angels of bliſs.

CHARLES V. EMPEROR.

CHARLES V. Emperor ſaid unto Sir Thomas Elliot then the king's ambaſſador in his court, after he had heard of Biſhop Fiſher and Sir Thomas More's ſufferings; on a time he ſpoke of it to Sir Thomas Elliot, who ſeemed to excuſe the matter by making ſome doubt of the report, to whom the Emperor reply'd, " It is too " true; but if we had two ſuch lights in all our king- " doms, as theſe men were, we could rather have cho- " ſen to have loſt two of the beſt and ſtrongeſt towns in " all our empire, than ſuffer ourſelves to be deprived of " them, much leſs to endure to have them wrongfully " taken from us."

THOMAS MORE Eſq; the AUTHOR's Great-grandſon, concerning his UTOPIA.

THE book that carrieth the prize of all his other

Latin books, of witty invention, is his Utopia; he doth in it most lively and pleasantly paint forth such an exquisite platform, pattern, and example of a singular good common-wealth, as to the same, neither the Lacedaemonians, nor the Athenians, nor yet the best of all other, that of the Romans, is comparable, full prettily and probably devising the said country to be one of the countries of the new-found lands, declared to him in Antwerp, by Hythlodius a Portingal, and one of the sea-companions of Americus Vesputius, that first sought out and found those lands; such an excellent and absolute an estate of a common-wealth, that saving the people were unchristened, might seem to pass any estate and common-wealth, I will not say of the old nations by me before mentioned, but even of any other in our time. Many great learned men, as Budeus, and Joannes Paludanus, upon a fervent zeal wished, that some excellent divines might be sent thither to preach Christ's gospel; yea, there were here amongst us at home, sundry good men and learned divines very desirous to take the voyage to bring the people to the faith of Christ, whose manners they did so well like. And this said jolly invention of Sir THOMAS MORE's seemed to bear a good countenance of truth, not only for the credit Sir THOMAS was of in the world, but also for that about the same time many strange and unknown nations and countrys were discovered, such as our forefathers never knew.———

A LETTER
FROM
SIR THOMAS MORE
TO
PETER GILES,
CONCERNING
UTOPIA.

I AM almoſt aſhamed, my deareſt Peter Giles, to ſend you this book of the Utopian common-wealth, after almoſt a year's delay; whereas no doubt you look'd for it within ſix weeks: for as you know I had no occaſion for uſing my invention, or for taking pains to put things into any method, becauſe I had nothing to do, but to repeat exactly thoſe things that I heard Raphael relate in your preſence; ſo neither was their any occaſion given for a ſtudied eloquence; ſince as he delivered things to us of the ſudden, and in a careleſs ſtile, ſo he being, as you know, a greater maſter of the Greek, than of the Latin, the plainer my words are, they will reſemble his ſimplicity the more, and will be by conſequence the nearer to the truth; and that is all that I think lies on me, and it is indeed the only thing in which I thought myself concerned. I confess, I had very little left on me in this matter, for otherwise the inventing and ordering of such a scheme, would have put a man of an ordinary pitch, either of capacity, or of learning, to some pains, and have cost him some time; but if it had been necessary that this relation should have been made, not only truly, but eloquently, it could never have been performed by me, even after all the pains and time that I could have bestowed upon it. My part in it was so very small, that it could not give me much trouble, all that belonged to me being only to give a true and full account of the things that I had heard; but altho' this required so very little of my time; yet even that little was long denied me by my other affairs, which press much upon me: for while in pleading, and hearing, and in judging or composing of causes, in waiting on some men upon business, and others out of respect, the greatest part of the day is spent on other men's affairs, the remainder of it must be given to my family at home: so that I can reserve no part of it to myself, that is, to my study: I must talk with my wife, and chat with my children, and I have somewhat to say to my servants; for all these things I reckon as a part of business, except a man will resolve to be a stranger at home: and with whomsoever either nature, or chance, or choice has engaged a man, in any commerce, he must endeavour to make himself as acceptable to those about him, as he possibly can; using still such a temper in it, that he may not spoil them by an excessive gentleness, so that his servants may not become his masters. In such things as I have named to you, do, days, months and years slip away; what is then left for writing? And yet I have said nothing of that time that must go for sleep, or for meat: in which many do waste almost as much of their time, as in sleep, which consumes very near the half of our life; and indeed all the time which I can gain to myself, is that which I steal from my sleep and my meals; and because that is not much, I have made but a slow progress; yet because it is somewhat, I have at last got to an end of my Utopia, which I now send to you, and expect that after you have read it, you will let me know if you can put me in mind of any thing that has escaped me; for tho' I would think myself very happy, if I had but as much invention and learning as I know I have memory, which makes me generally depend much upon it, yet I do not rely so entirely on it, as to think I can forget nothing.

My servant, John Clement, has started some things that shake me: you know he was present with us, as I think he ought to be at every conversation that may be of use to him, for I promise myself great matters from the progress he has so early made in the Greek and Roman learning. As far as my memory serves me, the bridge over Anider at Amaurot, was 500 paces broad, according to Raphael's account; but John assures me, he spoke only of 300 paces; therefore I pray you recollect what you can remember of this, for if you agree with him, I will believe that I have been mistaken; but if you remember nothing of it, I will not alter what I have written, because it is according to the best of my remembrance: for as I will take care that there may be nothing falsly set down; so if there is any thing doubtful, tho' I may perhaps tell a lie, yet I am sure I will not make one; for I would rather pass for a good man than for a wise man: but it will be easy to correct this mistake, if you can either meet with Raphael himself, or know how to write to him.

I have another difficulty that presses me more, and makes your writing to him the more necessary: I know not whom I ought to blame for it, whether Raphael, you, or myself; for as we did not think of asking it, so neither did he of telling us, in what part of the new-found world Utopia is situated; this was such an omission that I would gladly redeem it at any rate: I am ashamed, that after I have told so many things concerning this island, I cannot let my readers know in what sea it lies. There are some among us that have a mighty desire to go thither, and in particular, one pious divine is very earnest on it, not so much out of a vain curiosity of seeing unknown countries, as that he may advance our religion, which is so happily begun to be planted there; and that he may do this regularly, he intends to procure a mission from the Pope, and to be sent thither as their Bishop. In such a case as this, he makes no scruple of aspiring to that character, and thinks it is the rather meritorious to be ambitious of it, when one desires it only for advancing the Christian religion, and not for any honour or advantage that may be had by it, but is acted merely by a pious zeal. Therefore I earnestly beg it of you, if you can possibly meet with Raphael, or if you know how to write to him, that you will be pleased to inform yourself of these things, that there may be no falshood left in my book, nor any important truth wanting. And perhaps it will not be unfit to let him see the book itself: for as no man can correct any errors that may be in it, so well as he; so by reading it, he will be able to give a more perfect judgment of it than he can do upon any discourse concerning it: and you will be likewise able to discover whether this undertaking of mine is acceptable to him or not; for if he intends to write a relation of his travels, perhaps he will not be pleased that I should prevent him, in that part that belongs to the Utopian common-wealth; since if I should do so, his book will not surprize the world with the pleasure which this new discovery will give the age. And I am so little fond of appearing in print upon this occasion, that if he dislikes it, I will lay it aside; and even tho' he should approve of it, I am not positively determined as to publishing of it. Men's tastes differ much; some are of so morose a temper, so sour a disposition, and make such absurd judgments of things, that men of chearful and lively tempers, who indulge their genius, seem much more happy, than those who waste their time and strength in order to the publishing some book, that tho' of itself it might be useful or pleasant, yet instead of being well received, will be sure to be either loathed at, or censured. Many know nothing of learning, and others despise it: a man that is accustomed to a coarse and hard stile, thinks every thing is rough that is not barbarous. Our trifling pretenders to learning, think all is slight that is not drest up in words that are worn out of use; some love only old things, and many like nothing but what is their own. Some are so sour that they can allow no jests, and others are so dull that they can endure nothing that is sharp; and some are as much afraid of any thing that is quick or lively, as a man bit with a mad dog is of water; others are so light and unsettled, that their thoughts change as quick as they do their postures: and some, when they meet in taverns, take upon them among their cups to pass censures very freely on all writers; and with a supercilious liberty to condemn every thing they do not like: in which they have the advantage that a bald man has, who can catch hold of another by the hair, while the other cannot return the like upon him. They are safe as it were of gun-shot, since there is nothing in them considerable enough to be taken hold of. And some are so unthankful, that even when they are well pleased with a book, yet they think they owe nothing to the author; and are like those rude guests, who after they have been well entertained at a good dinner, go away when they have glutted their appetites, without so much as thanking him that treated them. But who would put himself to the charge of making a feast for men of such nice palats, and so different tastes; who are so forgetful of the civilities that are done? But do you once clear those points with Raphael, and then it will be time enough to consider whether it be fit to publish it or not: for since I have been at the pains to write it, if he consents to the publishing it, I will follow my friend's advice, and chiefly yours. Farewel my dear Peter, commend me kindly to your good wife, and love me still as you use to do, for I assure you I love you daily more and more.

THE DISCOURSES

OF

RAPHAEL HYTHLODAY,

OF THE

BEST STATE

OF A

COMMON-WEALTH.

BOOK FIRST.

HENRY the Eighth, the unconquer'd King of England, a prince adorned with all the virtues that become a great monarch; having some differences of no small consequence with Charles the most serene Prince of Castile, sent me into Flanders, as his ambassador, for treating and composing matters between them. I was collegue and companion to that incomparable man Cuthbert Tonstal, whom the king made lately Master of the Rolls, with such an universal applause; of whom I will say nothing, not because I fear that the testimony of a friend will be suspected, but rather because his learning and virtues are greater than that they can be set forth with advantage by me, and they are so well known, that they need not my commendations, unless I would, according to the proverb, 'Shew the sun with a lanthorn.' Those that were appointed by the prince to treat with us, met us at Bruges, according to agreement; they were all worthy men. The Markgrave of Bruges was their head, and the chief man among them; but he that was esteemed the wisest, and that spoke for the rest, was George Temse the provost of Cassesee; both art and nature had concurred to make him eloquent: He was very learned in the law; and as he had a great capacity, so by a long practice in affairs, he was very dextrous at them. After we had met once and again, and could not come to an agreement, they went to Brussels for some days to receive the prince's pleasure. And since our business did admit of it, I went to Antwerp: while I was there, among many that visited me, there was one that was more acceptable to me than any other: Peter Giles born at Antwerp, who is a man of great honour, and of a good rank in his town; yet it is not such as he deserves: for I do not know if there be any where to be found a learneder and a better bred young man: for as he is both a very worthy person and a very knowing man; so he is so civil to all men, and yet so particularly kind to his friends, and is so full of candour and affection, that there is not perhaps above one or two to be found any where, that is in all respects so perfect a friend as he is: He is extraordinarily modest, there is no artifice in him; and yet no man has more of a prudent simplicity than he has: his conversation was so pleasant and so innocently chearful, that his company did in a great measure lessen any longings to go back to my country, and to my wife and children, which an absence of four months had quickned very much. One day as I was returning home from mass at St. Mary's, which is the chief church, and the most frequented of any in Antwerp, I saw him by accident talking with a stranger, that seemed past the flower of his age; his face was tanned, he had a long beard, and his cloak was hanging carelesly about him, so that by his looks and habit, I concluded he was a seaman. As soon as Peter saw me, he came and saluted me; and as I was returning his civility, he took me aside, and pointing to him with whom he had been discoursing, he said, Do you see that man? I was just thinking to bring him to you. I answered, he should have been very welcome on your account: And on his own too, replied he, if you knew the man, for there is none alive that can give you so copious an account of unknown nations and countries as he can do; which I know you very much desire. Then said I, I did not guess amiss, for at first sight I took him for a seaman: But you are much mistaken, said he, for he has not sailed as a seaman, but as a traveller, or rather as a philosopher; for this Raphael, who from his family carries the name of Hythloday, as he is not ignorant of the Latin tongue, so he is eminently learned in the Greek, having applied himself more particularly to that than to the former, because he had given himself much to philosophy, in which he knew that the Romans have left us nothing that is valuable, except what is to be found in Seneca and Cicero. He is a Portuguese by birth, and was so desirous of seeing the world, that he divided his estate among his brothers, and run fortunes with Americus Vesputius, and bore a share in three of his four voyages, that are now published; only he did not return with him in his last, but obtained leave of him almost by force, that he might be one of those four and twenty who were left at the farthest place at which they touched, in their last voyage to New Castile. The leaving him thus, did not a little gratify one that was more fond of travelling than of returning home, to be buried in his own country; for he used often to say, that the way to heaven was the same from all places; and he that had no grave, had the heavens still over him. Yet this disposition of mind had cost him dear, if God had not been very gracious to him; for after he, with five Castilians, had travelled over many countries, at last, by a strange good fortune, he got to Ceylon, and from thence to Calicut, and there he very happily found some Portuguese ships; and so, beyond all men's expectations, he came back to his own country. When Peter had said this to me, I thanked him for his kindness, in intending to give me the acquaintance of a man, whose conversation he knew would be so acceptable to me; and upon that Raphael and I embraced one another: and after those civilities were past, which are ordinary for strangers upon their first meeting, we went all to my house, and entering into the garden, sat down on a green bank, and entertained one another in discourse. He told us, that when Vesputius had sailed away, he and his companions that staid behind in New Castile, did by degrees insinuate themselves into the people of the country, meeting often with them, and treating them gently: and at last they grew not only to live among them without danger, but to converse familiarly with them; and got so far into the heart of a prince, whose name and country I have forgot, that he both furnished them plentifully with all things necessary, and also with the conveniencies of travelling; both boats when they went by water, and waggons when they travelled over land; and he sent with them a very faithful guide, who was to introduce and recommend them to such other princes as they had a mind to see: and after many days journey, they came to towns, and cities, and to commonwealths, that were both happily governed, and well peopled. Under the Aequator, and as far on both sides of it as the sun moves, there lay vast desarts that were parched with the perpetual heat of the sun; the soil was withered, all things look'd dismally, and all places were either quite uninhabited, or abounded with wild beasts and serpents, and some few men, that were neither less wild, nor less cruel than the beasts themselves. But as they went farther, a new scene opened, all things grew milder, the air less burning, the soil more verdant, and even the beasts were less wild: and at last there are nations, towns, and cities, that have not only mutual commerce among themselves, and with their neighbours, but trade both by sea and land, to very remote countries. There they found the conveniences of seeing many countries on all hands, for no ship went any voyage into which he and his companions were not very welcome. The first vessels that they saw were flat-bottomed, their sails were made of reeds and wicker woven close together, only some were made of leather; but afterwards they found ships made with round keels, and canvass sails, and in all things like our ships; and the seamen understood both astronomy and navigation. He got wonderfully into their favour, by shewing them the use of the needle, of which till then they were utterly ignorant; and whereas they sailed before with great caution, and only in summer time, now they count all seasons alike, trusting wholly to the loadstone, in which they are perhaps more secure than safe; so that there is reason to fear, that this discovery which was thought would prove so much to their advantage, may by their imprudence become an occasion of much mischief to them. But it were too long to dwell on all that he told us, he had observed in every place, it would be too great a digreſſion from our preſent purpoſe: and whatever is neceſſary to be told, chiefly concerning the wiſe and prudent inſtitutions that he obſerved among civilized nations, may perhaps be related by us on a more proper occaſion. We aſk'd him many queſtions concerning all theſe things, to which he anſwered very willingly; only we made no enquiries after monſters, than which nothing is more common; for every where one may hear of ravenous dogs and wolves, and cruel men-eaters; but it is not ſo eaſy to find ſtates that are well and wiſely governed.

But as he told us of many things that were amiſs in thoſe new-found nations, ſo he reckoned up not a few things, from which patterns might be taken for correcting the errors of theſe nations among whom we live; of which an account may be given, as I have already promiſed, at ſome other time; for at preſent I intend only to relate thoſe particulars that he told us of the manners and laws of the Utopians: But I will begin with the occaſion that led us to ſpeak of that common-wealth. After Raphael had diſcourſed with great judgment of the errors that were both among us and theſe nations, of which there was no ſmall number, and had treated of the wiſe inſtitutions both here and there, and had ſpoken as diſtinctly of the cuſtoms and government of every nation through which he had paſt, as if he had ſpent his whole life in it; Peter being ſtruck with admiration, ſaid, I wonder, Raphael, how it comes that you enter into no king's service, for I am sure there are none to whom you would not be very acceptable: for your learning and knowledge, both of men and things, is such that you would not only entertain them very pleasantly, but be of good use to them, by the examples that you could set before them, and the advices that you could give them; and by this means you would both serve your own interest, and be of great use to all your friends. As for my friends, answer'd he, I need not be much concerned, having already done all that was incumbent on me toward them; for when I was not only in good health, but fresh and young, I distributed that among my kindred and friends, which other people do not part with till they are old and sick; and then they unwillingly give among them, that which they can enjoy no longer themselves. I think my friends ought to rest contented with this, and not to expect that for their sakes I should enslave myself to any king whatsoever. Soft and fair, said Peter, I do not mean that you should be a slave to any king, but only that you should assist them, and be useful to them. The change of the word, said he, does not alter the matter. But term it as you will, replied Peter, I do not see any other way in which you can be so useful, both in private to your friends, and to the public, and by which you can make your own condition happier. Happier! answer'd Raphael, is that to be compassed in a way so abhorrent to my genius? Now I live as I will, to which I believe few courtiers can pretend: and there are so very many that court the favour of great men, that there will be no great loss, if they are not troubled either with me, or with others of my temper. Upon this, I said, I perceive Raphael that you neither desire wealth nor greatness; and indeed I value and admire such a man much more than I do any of the great men in the world. Yet I think you would do a thing well becoming so generous and so philosophical a soul as yours is, if you would apply your time and thoughts to public affairs, even though you may happen to find that a little uneasy to yourself; and this you can never do with so much advantage, as by being taken into the council of some great prince, and by setting him on to noble and worthy things, which I know you would do if you were in such a post; for the springs both of good and evil, flow over a whole nation, from the prince, as from a lasting fountain. So much learning as you have, even without practice in affairs; or so great a practice as you have had, without any other learning, would render you a very fit counsellor to any king whatsoever. You are doubly mistaken, said he, Mr. More, both in your opinion of me, and in the judgment that you make of things: for as I have not that capacity that you fancy to be in me; so if I had it, the public would not be one jot the better, when I had sacrificed my quiet to it. For most princes apply themselves more to warlike matters, than to the useful arts of peace; and in thefe I neither have any knowledge, nor do I much defire it: They are generally more fet on acquiring new kingdoms, right or wrong, than on governing thofe well that they have: and among the minifters of princes, there are none that either are not fo wife as not to need any affiftance, or at leaft that do not think themfelves fo wife, that they imagine they need none; and if they do court any, it is only thofe for whom the prince has much perfonal favour, whom by their fawnings and flatteries they endeavour to fix to their own interefts; and indeed nature has fo made us, that we all love to be flattered, and to pleafe ourfelves with our own notions. The old crow loves his young, and the ape his cubs. Now if in fuch a court, made up of perfons that envy all others, and do only admire themfelves, one fhould but propofe any thing that he had either read in hiftory, or obferved in his travels, the reft would think that the reputation of their wifdom would fink, and that their interefts would be much depreffed, if they could not run it down: and if all other things failed, then they would fly to this, That fuch or fuch things pleafed our anceftors, and it were well for us if we could but match them. They would fet up their reft on fuch an anfwer, as a fufficient confutation of all that could be faid; as if this were a great mifchief, that any fhould be found wifer than his anceftors: but tho' they willingly let go all the good things that were among thofe of former ages; yet if better things are propofed, they cover themfelves obftinately with this excufe, of reverence to paft times. I have met with thefe proud, morofe, and abfurd judgments of things in many places, particularly once in England. Was you ever there, faid I? Yes, I was, anfwered he, and ftaid fome months there, not long after the rebellion in the Weft was fuppreffed, with a great flaughter of the poor people that were engaged in it.

I was then much obliged to that reverend prelate John Morton archbifhop of Canterbury, cardinal, and chancellor of England; a man, faid he, Peter, (for Mr. More knows well what he was) that was not lefs venerable for his wifdom and virtues, than for the high character he bore: he was of a middle ftature, not broken with age; his looks begot reverence rather than fear; his converfation was eafy, but ferious and grave; he took pleafure fometimes to try the force of thofe that came as fuitors to him upon bufinefs, by fpeaking fharply, tho' decently to them, and by that he difcovered their fpirit and prefence of mind; with which he was much delighted, when it did not grow up to an impudence, as bearing a great refemblance to his own temper; and he looked on fuch perfons as the fitteft men for affairs. He fpoke both gracefully and weightily; he was eminently fkilled in the law, and had a vaft underftanding, and a prodigious memory: and thofe excellent talents with which nature had furnifhed him, were improved by study and experience. When I was in England, the king depended much on his councils, and the government seemed to be chiefly supported by him; for from his youth up, he had been all along practised in affairs; and having passed through many traverses of fortune, he had acquired to his great cost, a vast stock of wisdom: which is not soon lost, when it is purchased so dear. One day when I was dining with him, there happened to be at table one of the English lawyers, who took occasion to run out in a high commendation of the severe execution of justice upon thieves, who, as he said, were then hanged so fast, that there were sometimes twenty on one gibbet; and upon that he said, he could not wonder enough how it came to pass, that since so few escaped, there were yet so many thieves left who were still robbing in all places. Upon this, I who took the boldness to speak freely before the cardinal, said, there was no reason to wonder at the matter, since this way of punishing thieves, was neither just in itself, nor good for the public; for as the severity was too great, so the remedy was not effectual; simple theft not being so great a crime, that it ought to cost a man his life; and no punishment how severe soever, being able to restrain those from robbing, who can find out no other way of livelyhood; and in this, said I, not only you in England, but a great part of the world imitate some ill masters, that are readier to chastise their scholars, than to teach them. There are dreadful punishments enacted against thieves, but it were much better to make such good provisions, by which every man might be put in a method how to live, and so be preserved from the fatal necessity of stealing, and of dying for it. There has been care enough taken for that, said he, there are many handicrafts, and there is husbandry, by which they may make a shift to live, unless they have a greater mind to follow ill courses. That will not serve your turn, said I, for many lose their limbs in civil or forreign wars, as lately in the Cornish rebellion, and sometime ago in your wars with France, who being thus mutilated in the service of their king and country, can no more follow their old trades, and are too old to learn new ones: but since wars are only accidental things, and have intervals, let us consider those things that fall out every day. There is a great number of noblemen among you, that live not only idle themselves as drones, subsisting by other mens labours, who are their tenants, and whom they pare to the quick, and thereby raise their revenues; this being the only instance of their frugality, for in all other things they are prodigal, even to the beggaring of themselves: but besides this, they carry about with them a huge number of idle fellows, who never learned any art by which they may gain their living; and these, as soon as either their lord dies, or they themselves fall sick, are turned out of doors; for your lords are readier to feed idle people, than to take care of the sick; and often the heir is not able to keep together so great a family as the predecessor did: now when the stomachs of those that are thus turned out of doors, grow keen, they rob no less keenly; and what else can they do? for after that, by wandering about, they have worn out both their health and their cloaths, and are tattered, and look ghastly, men of quality will not entertain them, and poor men dare not do it; knowing that one who has been bred up to idleness and pleasure, and who was used to walk about with his sword and buckler, despising all the neighbourhood with an insolent scorn, as far below him, is not fit for the spade and mattock: nor will he serve a poor man for so small a hire, and in so low a diet as he can afford. To this he answered, this sort of men ought to be particularly cherished among us, for in them consists the force of the armies for which we may have occasion; since their birth inspires them with a nobler sense of honour, than is to be found among tradesmen or ploughmen. You may as well say, replied I, that you must cherish thieves on the account of wars, for you never will want the one, as long as you have the other; and as robbers prove sometimes gallant soldiers, so soldiers prove often brave robbers; so near an alliance there is between those two sorts of life. But this bad custom of keeping many servants, that is so common among you, is not peculiar to this nation. In France there is yet a more pestiferous sort of people, for the whole country is full of soldiers, that are still kept up in time of peace; if such a state of a nation can be called a peace: and these are kept in pay upon the same account that you plead for those idle retainers about noblemen: this being a maxim of those pretended statesmen, that it is necessary for the public safety, to have a good body of veteran soldiers ever in readiness. They think raw men are not to be depended on, and they sometimes seek occasions for making war, that they may train up their soldiers in the art of cutting throats, or as Sallust observed, for keeping their hands in use, that they may not grow dull by too long intermission. But France has learn'd to its cost, how dangerous it is to feed such beasts. The fate of the Romans, Carthaginians, and Syrians, and many other nations, and cities, which were both overturned, and quite ruined by those standing armies, should make others wiser: and the folly of this maxim of the French, appears plainly even from this, that their trained soldiers find your raw men prove often too hard for them; of which I will not say much, lest you may think I flatter the English nation. Every day's experience shews, that the mechanics in the towns, or the clowns in the country, are not affraid of fighting with those idle gentlemen, if they are not disabled by some misfortune in their body, or dispirited by extreme want, so that you need not fear, that those well-shaped and strong men, (for it is only such that noblemen love to keep about them, till they spoil them) who now grow feeble with ease, and are softened with their effeminate manner of life, would be less fit for action if they were well bred and well employed. And it seems very unreasonable, that for the prospect of war, which you need never have but when you please, you should maintain so many idle men, as will always disturb you in time of peace, which is ever to be more considered than war. But I do not think that this necessity of stealing, arises only from hence, there is another cause of it that is more peculiar to England. What is that? said the cardinal: The increase of pasture, said I, by which your sheep, that are naturally mild, and easily kept in order, may be said now to devour men, and unpeople, not only villages, but towns: for wherever it is found, that the sheep of any soil yield a softer and richer wool than ordinary, there the nobility and gentry, and even those holy men the abbots, not contented with the old rents which their farms yielded, nor thinking it enough that they living at their ease, do no good to the public, resolve to do it hurt instead of good. They stop the course of agriculture, inclose grounds, and destroy houses and towns, reserving only the churches, that they may lodge their sheep in them: and as if forests and parks had swallowed up too little soil, those worthy contrymen turn the best inhabited places into solitudes; for when any unsatiable wretch, who is a plague to his country, resolves to inclose many thousand acres of ground, the owners, as well as tenants, are turned out of their poffeffions, by tricks, or by main force, or being wearied out with ill ufage, they are forced to fell them. So thófe miferable people, both men and women, married, unmarried, old and young, with their poor but numerous families, (fince country bufinefs requires many hands) are all forced to change their feats, not knowing whither to go; and they muft fell for almoft nothing, their houfhold-ftuff, which could not bring them much money, even tho' they might ftay for a buyer: when that little money is at an end, for it will be foon fpent; what is left for them to do, but either to fteal, and fo be hanged, (God knows how juftly) or to go about and beg? and if they do this, they are put in prifon as idle vagabonds; whereas they would willingly work, but can find none that will hire them; for there is no more occafion for country labour, to which they have been bred, when there is no arable ground left. One fhepherd can look after a flock, which will ftock an extent of ground that would require many hands, if it were to be ploughed and reaped. This likewife raifes the price of corn in many places. The price of wool is alfo rifen, that the poor people who were wont to make cloth, are no more able to buy it; and this likewife makes many of them idle: for fince the increafe of pafture, God has punifhed the avarice of the owners, by a rot among the fheep, which has deftroyed vaft numbers of them, but had been more juftly laid

C

upon the owners themselves. But suppose the sheep should encrease ever so much, their price is not like to fall; since tho' they cannot be called a monopoly, because they are not engrossed by one person, yet they are in so few hands, and these are so rich, that as they are not prest to sell them sooner than they have a mind to it, so they never do it till they have raised the price as high as is possible. And on the same account it is, that the other kinds of cattle are so dear, and so much the more, because that many villages being pulled down, and all country-labour being much neglected, there are none that look after the breeding of them. The rich do not breed cattle as they do sheep, but buy them lean, and at low prices; and after they have fattened them on their grounds, they sell them again at high rates. And I do not think that all the inconveniences that this will produce, are yet observed; for as they sell the cattle dear, so if they are consumed faster than the breeding countries, from which they are brought, can afford them; then the stock must decrease, and this must needs end in a great scarcity; and by these means this your island, that seemed as to this particular, the happiest in the world, will suffer much by the cursed avarice of a few persons; besides that, the rising of corn makes all people lessen their families as much as they can; and what can those who are dismissed by them do, but either beg or rob? And to this last, a man of a great mind is much sooner drawn than to the former. Luxury likewise breaks in a-pace upon you, to set forward your poverty and misery; there is an excessive vanity in apparel, and great cost in diet; and that not only in noblemens families, but even among tradesmen, and among the farmers themselves, and among all ranks of persons. You have also many infamous houses, and besides those that are known, the taverns and ale-houses are no better; add to these, dice, cards, tables, foot-ball, tennis and coits, in which money runs fast away; and those that are initiated into them, must in conclusion betake themselves to robbing, for a supply. Banish those plagues, and give order that these who have dispeopled so much soil, may either rebuild the villages that they have pulled down, or let out their grounds to such as will do it: restrain those engrossings of the rich, that are as bad almost as monopolies; leave fewer occasions to idleness; let agriculture be set up again, and the manufacture of the wool be regulated, that so there may be work found for these companies of idle people, whom want forces to be thieves, or who now being idle vagabonds, or useless servants, will certainly grow thieves at last. If you do not find a remedy to these evils, it is a vain thing to boast of your severity of punishing theft; which tho' it may have the appearance of justice, yet in itself it is neither just nor convenient: for if you suffer your people to be ill educated, and their manners to be corrupted from their infancy, and then punish them for those crimes to which their first education disposed them, what else is to be concluded from this, but that you first make thieves, and then punish them?

While I was talking thus, the counsellor that was present had prepared an answer, and had resolved to resume all I had said, according to the formality of a debate, in which things are generally repeated more faithfully than they are answered; as if the chief trial that were to be made, were of mens memories. So he said to me, you have talked prettily for a stranger, having heard of many things among us, which you have not been able to consider well; but I will make the whole matter plain to you, and will first repeat in order all that you have said, then I will shew how much the ignorance of our affairs has misled you, and will in the last place, answer all your arguments. And that I may begin where I promised, there were four things——Hold your peace, said the cardinal, for you will not have done soon that begin thus; therefore we will at present ease you of the trouble of answering, and reserve it to our next meeting, which shall be to-morrow, if Raphael's affairs and yours can admit of it: But, Raphael, said he to me, I would gladly know of you upon what reason it is that you think theft ought not to be punished by death? would you give way to it? or do you propose any other punishment that will be more useful to the public? For since death does not reftrain theft, if men thought their lives would be fafe, what fear or force could reftrain ill men? On the contrary, they would look on the mitigation of the punifhment, as an invitation to commit more crimes. I anfwered, it feems to me a very unjuft thing to take away a man's life for a little money; for nothing in the world can be of equal value with a man's life: and if it is faid, that it is not for the money that one fuffers, but for his breaking the law; I muft fay, extreme juftice is an extreme injury: for we ought not to approve of thefe terrible laws that make the fmalleft offences capital; nor of that opinion of the Stoicks that makes all crimes equal, as if there were no difference to be made between the killing a man, and the taking his purfe; between which, if we examine things impartially, there is no likenefs nor proportion. God has commanded us not to kill, and fhall we kill fo eafily for a little money? But if one fhall fay, that by that law we are only forbid to kill any, except when the laws of the land allow of it; upon the fame grounds, laws may be made to allow of adultery and perjury in fome cafes: for God having taken from us the right of difpofing, either of our own, or of other people's lives, if it is pretended that the mutual confent of men in making laws, allowing of manflaughter in cafes in which God has given us no example, frees people from the obligation of the divine law, and fo makes murder a lawful action; What is this, but to give a preference to human laws before the divine? And, if this is once admitted, by the same rule men may in all other things put what restrictions they please upon the laws of God. If by the Mosaical law, tho' it was rough and severe, as being a yoke laid on an obstinate and servile nation, men were only fined, and not put to death for theft; we cannot imagine that in this new law of mercy, in which God treats us with the tenderness of a father, he has given us a greater licence to cruelty, than he did to the Jews. Upon these reasons it is, that I think the putting thieves to death is not lawful; and it is plain and obvious that it is absurd, and of ill consequence to the commonwealth, that a thief and a murderer should be equally punished: for if a robber sees that his danger is the same, if he is convicted of theft, as if he were guilty of murder, this will naturally set him on to kill the person whom otherwise he would only have robbed, since, if the punishment is the same, there is more security, and less danger of discovery, when he that can best make it is put out of the way; so that the terrifying thieves too much, provokes them to cruelty.

But as to the question, What more convenient way of punishment can be found? I think it is much easier to find out that, than to invent any thing that is worse; Why should we doubt but the way that was so long in use among the old Romans, who understood so well the arts of government, was very proper for their punishment? they condemned such as they found guilty of great crimes, to work their whole lives in quarries, or to dig in mines with chains about them. But the method that I liked best, was that which I observed in my travels in Persia, among the Polylerites, who are a considerable and well-govern'd people. They pay a yearly tribute to the king of Persia; but in all other respects they are a free nation, and governed by their own laws. They lie far from the sea, and are environed with hills; and being contented with the productions of their own country, which is very fruitful, they have little commerce with any other nation; and as they, according to the genius of their country, have no appetite of enlarging their borders; so their mountains, and the pension that they pay to the Persian, secure them from all invasions. Thus they have no wars among them; they live rather conveniently than splendidly, and may be rather called a happy nation, than either eminent or famous; for I do not think that they are known so much as by name to any but their next neighbours. Those that are found guilty of theft among them, are bound to make restitution to the owner, and not as it is in other places, to the prince, for they reckon that the prince has no more right to the stolen goods than the thief; but if that which was stolen is no more in being, then the goods of the thieves are estimated, and restitution being made out of them, the remainder is given to their wives and children: and they themselves are condemned to serve in the public works, but are neither imprisoned, nor chained, unless there happened to be some extraordinary circumstances in their crimes. They go about loose and free, working for the public: If they are idle or backward to work, they are whipp'd; but if they work hard, they are well used and treated without any mark of reproach, only the lists of them are called always at night, and then they are shut up, and they suffer no other uneasiness, but this of constant labour; for as they work for the public, so they are well entertained out of the public stock, which is done differently in different places: In some places, that which is bestowed on them, is raised by a charitable contribution; and tho' this way may seem uncertain, yet so merciful are the inclinations of that people, that they are plentifully supplied by it; but in other places, public revenues are set aside for them; or there is a constant tax of a poll-money raised for their maintenance. In some places they are set to no public work, but every private man that has occasion to hire workmen, goes to the market-places and hires them of the public, a little lower than he would do a free-man: if they go lazily about their task, he may quicken them with the whip. By this means there is always some piece of work or other to be done by them; and besides their livelihood, they earn somewhat still to the public. They wear all a peculiar habit, of one certain colour, and their hair is cropt a little above their ears, and a little of one of their ears is cropt off. Their friends are allowed to give them either meat, drink, or cloaths, so they are of their proper colour; but it is death, both to the giver and taker, if they give them money; nor is it less penal for any free-man to take money from them, upon any account whatsoever: and it is also death for any of these slaves (so they are called) to handle arms. Those of every division of the country, are distinguished by a peculiar mark: and it is capital to lay that aside, and so it is also to go out of their bounds, or to talk with a slave of another jurisdiction; and the very attempt of an escape, is no less penal than an escape itself; it is death for any other slave to be accessory to it: if a free-man engages in it, he is condemned to slavery: those that discover it are rewarded; if free-men, in money; and if slaves, with liberty, together with a pardon for being accessory to it; that so they may find their account, rather in repenting of their accession to such a design, than in persisting in it.

These are their laws and rules in this matter; in which both the gentleness and advantages of them are very obvious; since by these means, as vices are destroyed, so men are preserved; but are so treated, that they see the necessity of being good: and by the rest of their life they make reparation for the mischief they had formerly done. Nor is there any hazard of their falling back to their old cuſtoms: And ſo little do travellers apprehend miſchief from them, that they generally make uſe of them for guides, from one juriſdiction to another; for there is nothing left them by which they can rob, or be the better for it, ſince as they are diſarmed, ſo the very having of money is a ſufficient conviction: and as they are certainly puniſhed if diſcovered, ſo they cannot hope to eſcape: for their habit being in all the parts of it different from what is commonly worn, they cannot fly away, unleſs they ſhould go naked, and even then their crop'd ear would betray them. The only danger to be fear'd from them is their conſpiring againſt the government: but thoſe of one diviſion or neighbourhood can do nothing to any purpoſe, unleſs a general conſpiracy were laid amongſt all the ſlaves of the ſeveral juriſdictions, which cannot be done, ſince they cannot meet or talk together; nor will any venture on a deſign where the concealment would be ſo dangerous, and the diſcovery ſo profitable: and none of them is quite hopeleſs of recovering his freedom, ſince by their obedience and patience, and by giving grounds to believe that they will change their manner of life for the future, they may expect at laſt to obtain their liberty: and ſome are every year reſtored to it, upon the good character that is given of them. When I had related all this, I added, that I did not ſee why ſuch a method might not be followed with more advantage, than could ever be expected from that ſevere justice which the counsellor magnified so much. To all this he answered, that it could never be so settled in England, without endangering the whole nation by it; and as he said that, he shook his head, and made some grimaces, and so held his peace; and all the company seemed to be of his mind: only the cardinal said, it is not easy to guess whether it would succeed well or ill, since no trial has been made of it: but if when the sentence of death were past upon a thief, the prince would reprieve him for a while, and make the experiment upon him, denying him the privilege of a sanctuary; then if it had a good effect upon him, it might take place; and if it succeeded not, the worst would be, to execute the sentence on the condemned person at last. And I do not see, said he, why it would be either unjust or inconvenient, or at all dangerous, to admit of such a delay: and I think the vagabonds ought to be treated in the same manner, against whom tho' we have made many laws, yet we have not been able to gain our end by them all. When the cardinal had said this, then they all fell to commend the motion, tho' they had despised it when it came from me; but they did more particularly commend that concerning the vagabonds, because it had been added by him.

I do not know whether it be worth the while to tell what followed, for it was very ridiculous; but I shall venture at it, for as it is not foreign to this matter, so some good use may be made of it. There was a jester standing by, that counterfeited the fool so naturally, that he seemed to be really one. The jests at which he offered were so cold and dull, that we laughed more at him than at them; yet sometimes he said, as it were by chance, things that were not unpleasant; so as to justify the old proverb, 'That he who throws 'the dice often, will sometimes have a lucky hit.' When one of the company had said, that I had taken care of the thieves, and the cardinal had taken care of the vagabonds, so that there remained nothing but that some public provision might be made for the poor, whom sickness or old age had disabled from labour: Leave that to me, said the fool, and I shall take care of them; for there is no sort of people whose sight I abhor more, having been so often vexed with them, and with their sad complaints; but as dolefully soever as they have told their tale to me, they could never prevail so far as to draw one penny of money from me: for either I had no mind to give them any thing, or, when I had a mind to it, I had nothing to give them: and they now know me so well, that they will not lose their labour on me, but let me pass without giving me any trouble, because they hope for nothing from me, no more in faith than if I were a priest: But I would have a law made, for sending all these beggars to monasteries, the men to the Benedictines to be lay-brothers, and the women to be nuns. The cardinal smiled, and approved of it in jest; but the rest liked it in earnest. There was a divine present, who tho' he was a grave, morose man, yet he was so pleased with this reflection that was made on the priests and the monks, that he began to play with the fool, and said to him, this will not deliver you from all beggars, except you take care of us friars. That is done already, answered the fool, for the cardinal has provided for you, by what he proposed for the restraining vagabonds, and setting them to work, for I know no vagabonds like you. This was well entertained by the whole company, who looking at the cardinal, perceived that he was not ill pleased at it; only the friar himself was so bit, as may be easily imagined, and fell out into such a passion, that he could not forbear railing at the fool, and called him knave, slanderer, backbiter, and son of perdition, and cited some dreadful threatnings out of the scriptures against him. Now the jester thought he was in his element, and laid about him freely: he said, good friar, be not angry, for it is written, " In patience possess your soul." The friar answered, (for I shall give you his own words) I am not angry, you hangman; at least I do not sin in it, for the Psalmist says, " Be ye angry, and sin not." Upon this the cardinal admonished him gently, and wished him to govern his passions. No, my lord, said he, I speak not but from a good zeal, which I ought to have; for holy men have had a good zeal, as it is said, " The zeal of thy house hath eaten me up;" and we sing in our church, that those who mock'd Elisha as he went up to the house of God, felt the effects of his zeal; which that mocker, that rogue, that scoundrel, will perhaps feel. You do this perhaps with a good intention said the cardinal; but, in my opinion, it were wiser in you, not to say better for you, not to engage in so ridiculous a contest with a fool. No, my lord, answered he, that were not wisely done; for Solomon, the wisest of men, said, "Answer a fool according to "his folly;" which I now do, and shew him the ditch into which he will fall, if he is not aware of it; for if the many mockers of Elisha, who was but one bald man, felt the effect of his zeal, what will become of one mocker of so many friars, among whom there are so many bald men? We have likewise a bull, by which all that jeer us are excommunicated. When the cardinal saw that there was no end of this matter, he made a sign to the fool to withdraw, and turned the discourse another way; and soon after he rose from the table, and dismissing us, he went to hear causes.

Thus, Mr. More, I have run out into a tedious story, of the length of which I had been ashamed, if, as you earnestly begged it of me, I had not observed you to hearken to it, as if you had no mind to lose any part of it: I might have contracted it, but I resolved to give it you at large, that you might observe how those that had despised what I had proposed, no sooner perceived that the cardinal did not dislike it, but they prefently approved of it, and fawned fo on him, and flattered him to fuch a degree, that they in good earneft applauded thofe things that he only liked in jeft. And from hence you may gather, how little courtiers would value either me or my counfels.

To this I anfwered, you have done me a great kindnefs in this relation; for as every thing has been related by you, both wifely and pleafantly, fo you have made me imagine, that I was in my own country, and grown young again, by recalling that good cardinal into my thoughts, in whofe family I was bred from my childhood: and tho' you are upon other accounts very dear to me, yet you are the dearer, becaufe you honour his memory fo much: but after all this I cannot change my opinion, for I ftill think that if you could overcome that averfion which you have to the courts of princes, you might do a great deal of good to mankind, by the advices that you would give; and this is the chief defign that every good man ought to propofe to himfelf in living: for whereas your friend Plato thinks that then nations will be happy, when either philofophers become kings, or kings become philofophers; no wonder if we are fo far from that happinefs, if philofophers will not think it fit for them to affift kings with their counfels. They are not fo bafe minded, faid he, but that they would willingly do it: many of them have already done it by their books, if thefe that are in power would hearken to their good advices. But Plato judged right, that except kings themselves became philosophers, it could never be brought about, that they who from their childhood are corrupted with false notions, should fall in intirely with the councils of philosophers, which he himself found to be true in the person of Dionysius.

Do not you think, that if I were about any king, and were proposing good laws to him, and endeavouring to root out of him all the cursed seeds of evil that I found in him, I should either be turned out of his court, or at least be laughed at for my pains? for instance, what could I signify if I were about the King of France, and were called into his cabinet-council, where several wise men do in his hearing propose many expedients; as by what arts and practices Milan may be kept; and Naples, that has so oft slip'd out of their hands, recovered; and how the Venetians, and after them the rest of Italy may be subdued; and then how Flanders, Brabant, and all Burgundy, and some other kingdoms which he has swallowed already in his designs, may be added to his empire. One proposes a league with the Venetians, to be kept as long as he finds his account in it, and that he ought to communicate councils with them, and give them some share of the spoil, till his success makes him need or fear them less, and then it will be easily taken out of their hands. Another proposes the hiring the Germans, and the securing the Switzers by pensions. Another proposes the gaining the Emperor by money, which is omnipotent with him. Another propofes a peace with the King of Arragon, and in order to the cementing it, the yielding up the King of Navarre's pretenfions. Another thinks the Prince of Caftile is to be wrought on, by the hope of an alliance; and that fome of his courtiers are to be gained to the French faction by penfions. The hardeft point of all is what to do with England: A treaty of peace is to be fet on foot, and if their alliance is not to be depended on, yet it is to be made as firm as can be; and they are to be called friends, but fufpected as enemies: therefore the Scots are to be kept in readinefs, to be let loofe upon England on every occafion; and fome banifhed nobleman is to be fupported underhand, (for by the league it cannot be done avowedly) who has a pretenfion to the crown, by which means that fufpected prince may be kept in awe. Now when things are in fo great a fermentation, and fo many gallant men are joining councils, how to carry on the war, if fo mean a man as I am fhould ftand up, and wifh them to change all their counfels, to let Italy alone, and ftay at home, fince the kingdom of France was indeed greater than that it could be well governed by one man; fo that he ought not to think of adding others to it: and if after this, I fhould propofe to them the refolutions of the A'chorians, a people that lie over againft the ifle of Utopia to the fouth eaft, who having long ago engaged in a war,

E

that they might gain another kingdom to their king, who had a pretenſion to it by an old alliance, by which it had deſcended to him; and having conquered it, when they found that the trouble of keeping it, was equal to that of gaining it; for the conquered people would be ſtill apt to rebel, or be expoſed to foreign invaſions, ſo that they muſt always be in war, either for them or againſt them; and that therefore they could never diſband their army: that in the mean time taxes lay heavy on them, that money went out of the kingdom; that their blood was ſacrificed to their king's glory, and that they were nothing the better by it, even in time of peace; their manners being corrupted by a long war; robbing and murders abounding every where, and their laws falling under contempt, becauſe their king being diſtracted with the cares of the kingdom, was leſs able to apply his mind to any one of them; when they ſaw there would be no end of thoſe evils, they by joint councils made an humble addreſs to their king, deſiring him to chooſe which of the two kingdoms he had the greateſt mind to keep, ſince he could not hold both; for they were too great a people to be governed by a divided king, ſince no man would willingly have a groom that ſhould be in common between him and another. Upon which the good prince was forced to quit his new kingdom to one of his friends, (who was not long after dethroned) and to be contented with his old one. To all this I would add, that after all thofe warlike attempts, and the vaft confufions, with the confumptions both of treafure and of people that muft follow them; perhaps upon fome misfortune, they might be forced to throw up all at laft; therefore it feemed much more eligible that the king fhould improve his antient kingdom all he could, and make it flourifh as much as was poffible; that he fhould love his people, and be beloved of them; that he fhould live among them, and govern them gently; and that he fhould let other kingdoms alone, fince that which had fallen to his fhare was big enough, if not too big for him. Pray how do you think would fuch a fpeech as this be heard? I confefs, faid I, I think not very well.

But what, faid he, if I fhould fort with another kind of minifters, whofe chief contrivances and confultations were, by what art treafure might be heaped up? Where one propofes the crying up of money, when the king had a great debt on him, and the crying it down as much when his revenues were to come in, that fo he might both pay much with a little, and in a little receive a great deal: another propofes a pretence of a war, that fo money may be raifed in order to the carrying it on, and that a peace might be concluded as foon as that was done; and this was to be made up with fuch appearances of religion as might work on the people, and make them impute it to the piety of their prince, and to his tendernefs of the lives of his subjects. A third offers some old musty laws, that have been antiquated by a long disuse; and which, as they had been forgotten by all the subjects, so they had been also broken by them; and that the levying of the penalties of these laws, as it would bring in a vast treasure, so there might be a very good pretence for it, since it would look like the executing of law, and the doing of justice. A fourth proposes the prohibiting of many things under severe penalties, especially such things as were against the interest of the people, and then the dispensing with these prohibitions upon great compositions, to those who might make advantages by breaking them. This would serve two ends, both of them acceptable to many; for as those whose avarice led them to transgress, would be severely fined; so the selling licenses dear, would look as if a prince were tender of his people, and would not easily, or at low rates, dispense with any thing that might be against the public good. Another proposes, that the judges must be made sure, that they may declare always in favour of the prerogative, that they must be often sent for to court, that the king may hear them argue those points in which he is concerned; since that how unjust soever any of his pretensions may be, yet still some one or other of them, either out of contradiction to others, or the pride of singularity, or that they may make their court, would find out some pretence or other to give the king a fair colour to carry the point: for if the judges but differ in opinion, the cleareſt thing in the world is made by that means diſputable, and truth being once brought in queſtion, the king upon that may take advantage to expound the law for his own profit: The judges that ſtand out will be brought over, either out of fear or modeſty; and they being thus gained, all of them may be ſent to the bench to give ſentence boldly, as the king would have it: for fair pretences will never be wanting when ſentence is to be given in the prince's favour: it will either be ſaid, that equity lies of his ſide, or ſome words in the law will be found ſounding that way, or ſome forced ſenſe will be put on them; and when all other things fail, the king's undoubted prerogative will be pretended, as that which is above all law; and to which a religious judge ought to have a ſpecial regard. Thus all conſent to that maxim of Craſſus, that a prince cannot have treaſure enough, ſince he muſt maintain his armies out of it: that a king, even tho' he would, can do nothing unjuſtly: that all property is in him, not excepting the very perſons of his ſubjects: and that no man has any other property, but that which the king out of his goodneſs thinks fit to leave him: and they think it is the prince's intereſt, that there be as little of this left as may be, as if it were his advantage that his people ſhould have neither riches nor liberty; ſince theſe things make them leſs eaſy and tame to a cruel and unjuſt government; whereas neceſſity and poverty blunts them, makes them patient, and bears them down, and breaks that height of spirit, that might otherwise dispose them to rebel. Now what if after all these propositions were made, I should rise up and assert, that such councils were both unbecoming a king, and mischievous to him: and that not only his honour, but his safety consisted more in his people's wealth, than in his own; if I should shew, that they choose a king for their own sake, and not for his; that by his care and endeavours they may be both easy and safe; and that therefore a prince ought to take more care of his people's happiness, than of his own, as a shepherd is to take more care of his flock than of himself. It is also certain, that they are much mistaken, that think the poverty of a nation is a means of the public safety: Who quarrel more than beggars do? Who does more earnestly long for a change, than he that is uneasy in his present circumstances? And who run in to create confusions with so desperate a boldness, as those who having nothing to lose, hope to gain by them? If a king should fall under so much contempt or envy, that he could not keep his subjects in their duty, but by oppression and ill usage, and by impoverishing them, it were certainly better for him to quit his kingdom, than to retain it by such methods, by which tho' he keeps the name of authority, yet he loses the majesty due to it. Nor is it so becoming the dignity of a king to reign over beggars, as to reign over rich and happy subjects. And therefore Fabritius, that was a man of a noble and exalted temper, said, he would rather govern rich men, than be rich himself; and for one man to abound in wealth and pleasure, when all about him are mourning and groaning, is to be a goaler and not a king: he is an unskilful physician, that cannot cure a disease, but by casting his patient into another: so he that can find no other way for correcting the errors of his people, but by taking from them the conveniencies of life, shews that he knows not what it is to govern a free nation. He himself ought rather to shake off his sloth, or to lay down his pride; for the contempt or hatred that his people have for him, takes its rise from the vices in himself. Let him live upon what belongs to himself, without wronging others, and accommodate his expence to his revenue. Let him punish crimes, and by his wise conduct let him endeavour to prevent them, rather than be severe when he has suffered them to be too common: Let him not rashly revive laws that are abrogated by disuse, especially if they have been long forgotten, and never wanted. And let him never take any penalty for the breach of them, to which a judge would not give way in a private man, but would look on him as a crafty and unjust person for pretending to it. To these things I would add, that law among the Macarians, that lie not far from Utopia, by which their king, in the day on which he begins to reign, is tied by an oath confirmed by solemn sacrifices, never to have at once above a thousand pounds of gold in his treasures, or so much silver as is equal to that in value. This law, as they say, was made by an excellent king, who had more regard to the riches of his country, than to his own wealth; and so provided against the heaping up of so much treasure, as might impoverish the people: he thought that moderate sum might be sufficient for any accident; if either the king had occasion for it against rebels, or the kingdom against the invasion of an enemy, but that it was not enough to encourage a prince to invade other men's rights, which was the chief cause of his making that law. He also thought, that it was a good provision for a free circulation of money, that is necessary for the course of commerce and exchange: and when a king must distribute all these extraordinary accessions that increase treasure beyond the due pitch, it makes him less disposed to oppress his subjects. Such a king as this is, will be the terror of ill men, and will be beloved of all good men.

If, I say, I should talk of these or such like things, to men that had taken their bias another way, how deaf would they be to it all? No doubt, very deaf, answered I; and no wonder, for one is never to offer at propositions or advices, that he is certain will not be entertained. Discourses so much out of the road could not avail any thing, nor have any effect on men, whose minds were prepossessed with different sentiments. This philosophical way of speculation, is not unpleasant among friends in a free converſation, but there is no room for it in the courts of princes, where great affairs are carried on by authority. That is what I was ſaying, replied he, that there is no room for philoſophy in the courts of princes. Yes, there is, ſaid I, but not for this ſpeculative philoſophy, that makes every thing to be alike fitting at all times: But there is another philoſophy that is more pliable, that knows its proper ſcene, and accommodates itſelf to it; and that teaches a man to act that part which has fallen to his ſhare, fitly and decently. If, when one of Plautus's comedies is upon the ſtage, and a company of ſervants are acting their parts, you ſhould come out in the garb of a philoſopher, and repeat out of Octavia, a diſcourſe of Seneca's to Nero, had it not been better for you to have ſaid nothing, than by mixing things of ſuch different natures, to have made ſuch an impertinent tragi-comedy? for you ſpoil and corrupt the play that is in hand, when you mix with it things diſagreeing to it, even tho' they were better than it is: therefore go through with the play that is acting the beſt you can; and do not confound it, becauſe another that is pleaſanter comes into your thoughts. It is even ſo in a commonwealth, and in the councils of princes; if ill opinions cannot be quite rooted out; and if you cannot cure ſome received vices according to your wiſhes, you muſt not therefore abandon the common-wealth; or forſake the ſhip in a ſtorm, becauſe you cannot command the

F

winds; nor ought you to affault people with difcourfes that are out of their road, when you fee their notions are fuch that you can make no impreffion on them: but you ought to caft about, and as far as you can to manage things dexteroufly, that fo if you cannot make matters go well, they may be as little ill as is poffible; for except all men were good, all things cannot go well; which I do not hope to fee in a great while. By this, anfwered he, all that I fhall do fhall be to preferve myfelf from being mad, while I endeavour to cure the madnefs of other people: for, if I will fpeak truth, I muft fay fuch things as I was formerly faying; and for lying, whether a philofopher can do it or not, I cannot tell; I am fure I cannot do it. But tho' thefe difcourfes may be uneafy and ungrateful to them, I do not fee why they fhould feem foolifh or extravagant: indeed if I fhould either propofe fuch things as Plato has contrived in his Common-wealth, or as the Utopians practife in theirs, tho' they might feem better, as certainly they are, yet they are fo quite different from our eftablifhment, which is founded on property, there being no fuch thing among them, that I could not expect that it fhould have any effect on them: but fuch difcourfes as mine, that only call paft evils to mind, and give warning of what may follow, have nothing in them that is fo abfurd, that they may not be ufed at any time; for they can only be unpleafant to thofe who are refolved to run headlong the contrary way: and if we muſt let alone every thing as abſurd or extravagant, which by reaſon of the wicked lives of many, may ſeem uncouth, we muſt, even among chriſtians, give over preſſing the greateſt part of thoſe things that Chriſt hath taught us: tho' he has commanded us not to conceal them, but to proclaim on the houſe tops that which he taught in ſecret. The greateſt parts of his precepts are more diſagreeing to the lives of the men of this age, than any part of my diſcourſe has been: but the preachers ſeem to have learned that craft to which you adviſe me; for they obſerving that the world would not willingly ſuit their lives to the rules that Chriſt has given, have fitted his doctrine, as if it had been a leaden rule, to their lives; that ſo ſome way or other they might agree with one another. But I ſee no other effect of this compliance, except it be that men become more ſecure in their wickedneſs by it. And this is all the ſucceſs that I can have in a court; for I muſt always differ from the reſt, and then I will ſignify nothing; or if I agree with them, then I will only help forward their madneſs. I do not comprehend what you mean by your caſting about, or by the bending and handling things ſo dexterouſly, that if they go not well, they may go as little ill as may be: for in courts they will not bear with a man's holding his peace, or conniving at them: a man muſt bare-facedly approve of the worſt councils, and conſent to the blackeſt deſigns: ſo that one would paſs for a spy, or possibly for a traytor, that did but coldly approve of such wicked practices: And when a man is engaged in such a society, he will be so far from being able to mend matters by his casting about, as you call it, that he will find no occasions of doing any good: the ill company will sooner corrupt him, than be the better for him: or if notwithstanding all their ill company, he remains still entire and innocent, yet their follies and knavery will be imputed to him; and by mixing councils with them, he must bear his share of all the blame that belongs wholly to others.

It was no ill simile, by which Plato set forth the unreasonableness of a philosopher's meddling with government: If one, says he, shall see a great company run out into the rain every day, and delight to be wet in it; and if he knows that it will be to no purpose for him to go and persuade them to come into their houses, and avoid the rain; so that all that can be expected from his going to speak to them, will be, that he shall be wet with them; when it is so, he does best to keep within doors, and preserve himself, since he cannot prevail enough to correct other people's folly.

Tho' to speak plainly what is my heart, I must freely own to you, that as long as there is any property, and while money is the standard of all other things, I cannot think that a nation can be governed either justly or happily: Not justly, because the best things will fall to the share of the worst men: Nor happily, becaufe all things will be divided among a few, (and even thefe are not in all refpects happy) the reft being left to be abfolutely miferable. Therefore when I reflect on the wife and good conftitutions of the Utopians, among whom all things are fo well governed, and with fo few laws; and among whom as virtue hath its due reward, yet there is fuch an equality, that every man lives in plenty; and when I compare with them fo many other nations that are ftill making new laws, and yet can never bring their conftitution to a right regulation, among whom tho' every one has his property; yet all the laws that they can invent, cannot prevail fo far, that men can either obtain or preferve it, or be certainly able to diftinguifh what is their own, from what is another man's; of which the many law-fuits that every day break out, and depend without any end, give too plain a demonftration: When, I fay, I ballance all thefe things in my thoughts, I grow more favourable to Plato, and do not wonder that he refolved, not to make any laws for fuch as would not fubmit to a community of all things: for fo wife a man as he was, could not but forefee that the fetting all upon the level, was the only way to make a nation happy: which cannot be obtained fo long as there is property: for when every man draws to himfelf all that he can compafs, by one title or another, it muft needs follow, that how plentiful foever a nation may be, yet a few dividing the wealth of it among themfelves, the reft muft fall under poverty. So that there will be two sorts of people among them, that deserve that their fortunes should be interchanged; the former being useless, but wicked and ravenous; and the latter, who by their constant industry serve the public more than themselves, being sincere and modest men. From whence I am persuaded, that till property is taken away, there can be no equitable or just distribution made of things, nor can the world be happily governed; for as long as that is maintained, the greatest and the far best part of mankind, will be still oppressed with a load of cares and anxieties. I confess, without the taking of it quite away, those pressures that lie on a great part of mankind, may be made lighter; but they can never be quite removed. For if laws were made, determining at how great an extent in soil, and at how much money every man must stop, and limiting the prince that he may not grow too great, and restraining the people that they may not become too insolent, and that none might factiously aspire to public employments; and that they might neither be sold, nor made burthensome by a great expence; since otherwise those that serve in them, will be tempted to reimburse themselves by cheats and violence, and it will become necessary to find out rich men for undergoing those employments for which wise men ought rather to be sought out; these laws, I say, may have such effects, as good diet and care may have on a sick man, whose recovery is desperate: they may allay and mitigate the difeafe, but it can never be quite healed, nor the body politic be brought again to a good habit, as long as property remains; and it will fall out as in a complication of difeafes, that by applying a remedy to one fore, you will provoke another; and that which removes the one ill fymptom produces others, while the ftrengthening of one part of the body weakens the reft. On the contrary, anfwered I, it feems to me that men cannot live conveniently, where all things are common: How can there be any plenty, where every man will excufe himfelf from labour: for as the hope of gain doth not excite him, fo the confidence he has in other men's induftry, may make him flothful: and if people come to be pinched with want, and yet cannot difpofe of any thing as their own; what can follow upon this, but perpetual fedition and bloodfhed, efpecially when the reverence and authority due to magiftrates falls to the ground? For I cannot imagine how that can be kept up among thofe that are in all things equal to one another. I do not wonder, faid he, that it appears fo to you, fince you have no notion, or at leaft no right one, of fuch a conftitution: but if you had been in Utopia with me, and had feen their laws and rules as I did, for the fpace of five years, in which I lived among them; and during which time I was fo delighted with them, that indeed I would never have left them, if it had not been to make the difcovery of that new world to the Europeans; you would then confefs that you had never feen a people fo well constituted as they are. You will not easily persuade me, said Peter, that any nation in that new world is better governed than those among us are. For as our understandings are not worse than theirs, so our government, if I mistake not, being antienter, a long practice has helped us to find out many conveniencies of life: and some happy chances have discovered other things to us, which no man's understanding could ever have invented. As for the antiquity, either of their government, or of ours, said he, you cannot pass a true judgment of it, unless you had read their histories; for if they are to be believed, they had towns among them, before these parts were so much as inhabited: and as for these discoveries, that have been either hit on by chance, or made by ingenious men, these might have happened there as well as here. I do not deny but we are more ingenious than they are, but they exceed us much in industry and application: they knew little concerning us, before our arrival among them; they call us all by a general name of the nations that lie beyond the equinoctial line; for their chronicle mentions a ship-wrack that was made on their coast 1200 years ago; and that some Romans and Egyptians that were in the ship, getting safe a shore, spent the rest of their days amongst them; and such was their ingenuity, that from this single opportunity, they drew the advantage of learning from those unlook'd-for guests, all the useful arts that were then among the Romans, which those ship-wrack'd men knew: and by the hints that they gave them, they themselves found out even some of those arts which they could not fully explain to them; so happily did they improve that accident, of having some of our people cast upon their shore: but if any such accident have at any time brought any from thence into Europe, we have been so far from improving it, that we do not so much as remember it; as in after times perhaps it will be forgot by our people that I was ever there. For though they from one such accident, made themselves masters of all the good inventions that were among us; yet I believe it would be long before we would learn or put in practice any of the good institutions that are among them: and this is the true cause of their being better governed, and living happier than we do, though we come not short of them in point of understanding or outward advantages. Upon this I said to him, I do earnestly beg of you, that you would describe that island very particularly to us. Be not too short in it, but set out in order all things relating to their soil, their rivers, their towns, their people, their manners, constitution, laws: and in a word, all that you imagine we desire to know: and you may well imagine that we desire to know every thing concerning them, of which we are hitherto ignorant. I will do it very willingly, said he, for I have digested the whole matter carefully; but it will take up some time. Let us go then, said I, first and dine,

G

and then we shall have leisure enough. Be it so, said he. So we went in and dined, and after dinner we came back, and sat down in the same place. I ordered my servants to take care that none might come and interrupt us: and both Peter and I desired Raphael to be as good as his word: So when he saw that we were very intent upon it, he paused a little to recollect himself, and began in this manner.

THE

SECOND BOOK.

THE island of Utopia, in the middle of it where it is broadest, is two hundred miles broad, and holds almost at the same breadth over a great part of it; but it grows narrower towards both ends. Its figure is not unlike a crescent: between its horns, the sea comes in eleven miles broad, and spreads itself into a great bay, which is environed with land to the compass of about five hundred miles, and is well secured from winds: there is no great current in the bay, and the whole coast is, as it were, one continued harbour, which gives all that live in the island great convenience for mutual commerce: but the entry into the bay, what by rocks on one hand, and shallows on the other, is very dangerous. In the middle of it there is one single rock which appears above water, and so is not dangerous; on the top of it there is a tower built, in which a garrison is kept. The other rocks lie under water, and are very dangerous. The channel is known only to the natives, so that if any stranger should enter into the bay, without one of their pilots, he would run a great danger of shipwreck: for even they themselves could not pass it safe, if some marks that are on their coast did not direct their way; and if these should be but a little shifted, any fleet that might come against them, how great soever it were, would be certainly lost. On the other side of the island, there are likewise many harbours; and the coast is so fortified, both by nature and art, that a small number of men can hinder the descent of a great army. But they report (and there remain good marks of it to make it credible) that this was no island at first, but a part of the continent. Utopus that conquered it (whose name it still carries, for Abraxa was its first name) and brought the rude and uncivilized inhabitants into such a good government, and to that measure of politeness, that they do now far excel all the rest of mankind; having soon subdued them, he designed to separate them from the continent, and to bring the sea quite about them, and in order to that he made a deep channel to be digged fifteen miles long: he not only forced the inhabitants to work at it, but likewise his own soldiers, that the natives might not think he treated them like slaves: and having set vast numbers of men to work, he brought it to a speedy conclusion beyond all mens expectations: By this their neighbours, who laughed at the folly of the undertaking at first, were struck with admiration and terror, when they saw it brought to perfection. There are fifty-four cities in the island, all large and well built: The manners, customs, and laws of all their cities are the same, and they are all contrived as near in the same manner as the ground on which they stand will allow:

the nearest lie at least twenty-four miles distance from one another, and the most remote are not so far distant, but that a man can go on foot in one day from it, to that which lies next it. Every city sends three of their wisest senators once a year to Amaurot, for consulting about their common concerns; for that is the chief town of the island, being situated near the center of it, so that it is the most convenient place for their assemblies. Every city has so much ground set off for its jurisdiction, that there is twenty miles of soil round it, assigned to it: and where the towns lie wider, they have much more ground: no town desires to enlarge their bounds, for they consider themselves rather as tenants than landlords of their soil. They have built over all the country, farm-houses for husbandmen, which are well contrived, and are furnished with all things necessary for country labour. Inhabitants are sent by turns from the cities to dwell in them; no country family has fewer than forty men and women in it, besides two slaves. There is a master and a mistress set over every family; and over thirty families there is a magistrate settled. Every year twenty of this family come back to the town, after they have stayed out two years in the country: and in their room there are other twenty sent from the town, that they may learn country work, from those that have been already one year in the country, which they must teach those that come to them the next year from the town,

By this means such as dwell in those country farms, are never ignorant of agriculture, and so commit no errors in it, which might otherwise be fatal to them, and bring them under a scarcity of corn. But tho' there is every year such a shifting of the husbandmen, that none may be forced against his mind to follow that hard course of life too long; yet many among them take such pleasure in it, that they desire leave to continue many years in it. These husbandmen labour the ground, breed cattle, hew wood, and convey it to the towns, either by land or water, as is most convenient. They breed an infinite multitude of chickens in a very curious manner: for the hens do not sit and hatch them, but they lay vast numbers of eggs in a gentle and equal heat, in which they are hatched; and they are no sooner out of the shell, and able to stir about, but they seem to consider those that feed them as their mothers, and follow them as other chickens do the hen that hatched them. They breed very few horses, but those they have, are full of mettle, and are kept only for exercising their youth in the art of sitting and riding of them; for they do not put them to any work, either of plowing or carriage, in which they employ oxen; for tho' horses are stronger, yet they find oxen can hold out longer; and as they are not subject to so many diseases, so they are kept upon a less charge, and with less trouble: and when they are so worn out, that they are no more fit for labour, they are good meat at last.

They sow no corn, but that which is to be their bread; for they drink either wine, cider, or perry, and often water, sometimes pure, and sometimes boiled with honey or liquorish, with which they abound: and tho' they know exactly well how much corn will serve every town, and all that tract of country which belongs to it, yet they sow much more, and breed more cattle than are necessary for their consumption: and they give that overplus of which they make no use, to their neighbours. When they want any thing in the country which it does not produce, they fetch that from the town, without carrying any thing in exchange for it: and the magistrates of the town take care to see it given them: for they meet generally in the town once a month, upon a festival day. When the time of harvest comes, the magistrates in the country send to those in the towns, and let them know how many hands they will need for reaping the harvest; and the number they call for being sent to them, they commonly dispatch it all in one day.

Of their Towns, particularly of AMAUROT.

HE that knows one of their towns, knows them all, they are so like one another, except where the situation makes some difference. I shall therefore describe one of them, and it is no matter which; but none is so proper as Amaurot: for as none is more eminent, all the rest yielding in precedence to this, because it is the seat of their supreme council; so there was none of them better known to me, I having lived five years altogether in it.

It lies upon the side of a hill, or rather a rising ground: its figure is almost square, for from the one side of it, which shoots up almost to the top of the hill, it runs down in a descent for two miles to the river Anider; but it is a little broader the other way that runs along by the bank of that river. The Anider rises about eighty miles above Amaurot, in a small spring at first; but other brooks falling into it, of which two are more considerable: as it runs by Amaurot, it is grown half a mile broad, but it still grows larger and larger, till after sixty miles course below it, it is buried in the ocean. Between the town and the sea, and for some miles above the town, it ebbs and flows every six hours, with a strong current. The tide comes up for about thirty miles so full, that there is nothing but salt water in the river, the fresh water being driven back with its force; and above that, for some miles, the water is brackish, but a little higher, as it runs by the town, it is quite fresh; and when the tide ebbs, it continues fresh all along to the sea. There is a bridge cast over the river, not of timber, but of fair stone, consisting of many stately arches; it lies at that part of the town which is farthest from the sea, so that ships without any hindrance lie all along the side of the town. There is likewise another river that runs by it, which tho' it is not great, yet it runs pleasantly, for it rises out of the same hill on which the town stands, and so runs down through it, and falls into the Anider. The inhabitants have fortified the fountain-head of this river, which springs a little without the town; that so if they should happen to be besieged, the enemy might not be able to stop or divert the course of the water, nor poison it; from thence it is carried in earthen pipes to the lower streets: and for those places of the town, to which the water of that small river cannot be conveyed, they have great cisterns for receiving the rain-water, which supplies the want of the other. The town is compassed with a high and thick wall, in which there are many towers and forts; there is also a broad and deep dry ditch, set thick with thorns, cast round three sides of the town, and the river is instead of a ditch on the fourth side. The streets are made very convenient for all carriage, and are well sheltered from the winds. Their buildings are good, and are so uniform, that a whole side of a street looks like one house. The streets are twenty foot broad; there lie gardens behind all their houses; these are large, but inclosed with buildings, that on all hands face the streets; so that every house has both a door to the street, and a back door to the garden: their doors have all two leaves, which as they are easily opened, so they shut of their own accord; and there being no property among them, every man may freely enter into any house whatsoever. At every ten years end, they shift their houses by lots. They cultivate their gardens with great care, so that they have both vines, fruits, herbs, and flowers in them; and all is so well ordered, and so finely kept, that I never saw gardens any where that were both so fruitful and so beautiful as theirs are. And this humour of ordering their gardens so well, is not only kept up by the pleasure they find in it, but also by an emulation between the inhabitants of the several streets, who vie with one another in this matter; and there is indeed nothing belonging to the whole town, that is both more useful, and more pleasant. So that he who founded the town, seems to have taken care of nothing more than of their gardens; for they say, the whole scheme of the town was designed at first by Utopus, but he left all that belonged to the ornament and improvement of it, to be added by those that should come after him, that being too much for one man to bring to perfection. Their records, that contain the history of their town and state, are preserved with an exact care, and run backwards 1760 years. From these it appears, that their houses were at first low and mean, like cottages, made of any sort of timber, and were built with mud walls, and thatch'd with straw: but now their houses are three stories high, the fronts of them are faced either with stone, plaistering, or brick; and between the facings of their walls, they throw in their rubbish; their roofs are flat, and on them they lay a sort of plaister which costs very little, and yet it is so tempered, that as it is not apt to take fire, so it resists the weather more than lead does. They have abundance of glass among them, with which they glaze their windows: they use also in their windows, a thin linen cloth, that is so oiled or gummed, that by that means it both lets in the light more freely to them, and keeps out the wind the better.

Of their Magistrates.

THIRTY families choose every year a magistrate, who was called anciently the Syphogrant, but is called the Philarch: and over every ten Syphogrants with the families subject to them, there is another magistrate, who was anciently called the Tranibore, but of late the Archphilarch. All the Syphogrants, who are in number 200, choose the Prince out of a list of four, whom the people of the four divisions of the city name to them, but they take an oath before they proceed to an election, that they will choose him whom they think meetest for the office: they give their voices secretly, so that it is not known for whom every one gives his suffrage. The Prince is for life, unless he is removed upon suspicion of some design to enslave the people. The Tranibors are new chosen every year, but yet they are for the most part still continued. All their other magistrates are only annual. The Tranibors meet every third day, and oftner if need be, and consult with the Prince, either concerning the affairs of the state in general, or such private differences as may arise sometimes among the people: tho' that falls out but seldom. There are always two Syphogrants called into the council-chamber, and these are changed every day. It is a fundamental rule of their government, that no conclusion can be made in any thing that relates to the public, till it has been first debated three several days in their council. It is death for any to meet and consult concerning the state, unless it be either in their ordinary council, or in the assembly of the whole body of the people.

These things have been so provided among them, that the Prince and the Tranibors may not conspire together to change the government, and enslave the people; and therefore when any thing of great importance is set on foot, it is sent to the Syphogrants; who after they have communicated it with the families that belong to their divisions, and have considered it among themselves, make report to the senate; and upon great occasions, the matter is referred to the council of the whole island. One rule observed in their council, is, never to debate a thing on the same day in which it is first proposed; for that is always referred to the next meeting, that so men may not rashly, and in the heat of discourse, engage themselves too soon, which may bias them so much, that instead of considering the good of the public, they will rather study to maintain their own notions; and by a perverse and preposterous sort of shame, hazard their country, rather than endanger their own reputation, or venture the being suspected to have wanted foresight in the expedients that they proposed at first. And therefore to prevent this, they take care that they may rather be deliberate, than sudden in their motions.

Of their Trades, and Manner of Life.

AGRICULTURE is that which is so universally understood among them all, that no person, either man or woman, is ignorant of it; from their childhood they are instructed in it, partly by what they learn at school, and partly by practice, they being led out often into the fields, about the town, where they not only see others at work, but are likewise exercised in it themselves. Besides agriculture, which is so common to them all, every man has some peculiar trade to which he applies himself, such as the manufacture of wool, or flax, masonry, smiths work, or carpenters work; for there is no other sort of trade that is in great esteem among them. All the island over, they wear the same sort of clothes without any other distinction, except that which is necessary for marking the difference between the two sexes, and the married and unmarried. The fashion never alters; and as it is not ungrateful nor uneasy, so it is fitted for their climate, and calculated both for their summers and winters. Every family makes their own clothes; but all among them, women as well as men, learn one or other of the trades formerly mentioned. Women, for the most part, deal in wool and flax, which suit better with their feebleness, leaving the other ruder trades to the men. Generally the same trade passes down from father to son, inclinations often following descent: But if any man's genius lies another way, he is by adoption translated into a family that deals in the trade to which he is inclined: and when that is to be done, care is taken not only by his father, but by the magistrate, that he may be put to a discreet and good man. And if after a man has learned one trade, he desires to acquire another, that is also allowed, and is managed in the same manner as the former. When he has learn'd both, he follows that which he likes best, unless the public has more occasion for the other.

The chief, and almost the only business of the Syphogrants, is to take care that no man may live idle, but that every one may follow his trade diligently: Yet they do not wear themselves out with perpetual toil, from morning to night, as if they were beasts of burden, which as it is indeed a heavy flavery; fo it is the common courfe of life of all tradesmen every where, except among the Utopians: But they, dividing the day and night into twenty-four hours, appoint fix of thefe for work, three of them are before dinner; and after that they dine, and interrupt their labour for two hours, and then they go to work again for other three hours; and after that they fup, and at eight a clock, counting from noon, they go to bed, and fleep eight hours: and for their other hours, befides thofe of work, and thofe that go for eating and fleeping, they are left to every man's difcretion; yet they are not to abufe that interval to luxury and idlenefs, but muft employ it in fome proper exercife according to their various inclinations, which is for the moft part reading. It is ordinary to have public lectures every morning before day-break; to which none are obliged to go, but thofe that are marked out for literature; yet a great many, both men and women of all ranks, go to hear lectures of one fort or another, according to the variety of their inclinations. But if others, that are not made for contemplation, choofe rather to employ themfelves at that time in their trade, as many of them do, they are not hindered, but are commended rather, as men that take care to ferve their country. After fupper, they fpend an hour in fome diverfion: in fummer it is in their gardens, and in winter it is in the halls where they eat; and they entertain themfelves in them, either with music or discourse. They do not so much as know dice, or such like foolish and mischievous games: they have two sorts of games not unlike our chess; the one is between several numbers, by which one number, as it were, consumes another: the other resembles a battle between the vices and the virtues, in which the enmity in the vices among themselves, and their agreement against virtue is not unpleasantly represented; together with the special oppositions between the particular virtues and vices; as also the methods by which vice does either openly assault, or secretly undermine virtue; and virtue on the other hand resists it; and the means by which either side obtains the victory. But this matter of the time set off for labour, is to be narrowly examined, otherwise you may perhaps imagine, that since there are only six hours appointed for work, they may fall under a scarcity of necessary provisions. But it is so far from being true, that this time is not sufficient for supplying them with a plenty of all things, that are either necessary or convenient; that it is rather too much; and this you will easily apprehend, if you consider how great a part of all other nations is quite idle. First, Women generally do little, who are the half of mankind; and if some few women are diligent, their husbands are idle: Then consider the great company of idle priests, and of those that are called religious men; add to these all rich men, chiefly those that have estates in lands, who are called noblemen and gentlemen, together with their families, made up of idle persons, that do nothing but go swaggering about: Reckon in with these, all those strong and lusty beggars, that go about pretending some disease, in excuse for their begging; and upon the whole account you will find, that the number of those by whose labours mankind is supplied; is much less than you did perhaps imagine: Then consider how few of those that work, are employed in labours that men do really need: for we who measure all things by money, give occasions to many trades that are both vain and superfluous, and that serve only to support riot and luxury. For if those who are at work, were employed only in such things as the conveniences of life require, there would be such an abundance of them, and by that means the prices of them would so sink, that tradesmen could not be maintained by their gains; if all those who labour about useless things, were set to more profitable trades; and if all that number that languishes out their life in sloth and idleness, of whom every one consumes as much as any two of the men that are at work do, were forced to labour, you may easily imagine that a small proportion of time would serve for doing all that is either necessary, profitable or pleasant to mankind, pleasure being still kept within its due bounds: which appears very plainly in Utopia, for there, in a great city, and in all the territory that lies round it, you can scarce find five hundred, either men or women, that by their age and ſtrength, are capable of labour, that are not engaged in it; even the ſyphogrants themſelves, tho' the law excuſes them, yet do not excuſe themſelves, that ſo by their examples they may excite the induſtry of the reſt of the people; the like exemption is allowed to thoſe, who being recommended to the people by the prieſts, are by the ſecret ſuffrages of the ſyphogrants, privileged from labour, that they may apply themſelves wholly to ſtudy; and if any of theſe fall ſhort of thoſe hopes that he ſeemed to give at firſt, he is obliged to go to work. And ſometimes a mechanic, that does ſo employ his leiſure hours, that he makes a conſiderable advancement in learning, is eaſed from being a tradeſman, and ranked among their learned men. Out of theſe they chooſe their ambaſſadors, their prieſts, their tranibors, and the prince himſelf; who was anciently called their Barzenes, but is called of late their Ademus.

And thus from the great numbers among them, that are neither ſuffered to be idle, nor to be employed in any fruitleſs labour; you may eaſily make the eſtimate, how much good work may be done in thoſe few hours in which they are obliged to labour. But beſides all that has been already ſaid, this is to be conſidered, that thoſe needful arts which are among them, are managed with leſs labour than any where elſe. The building, or the repairing of houſes among us, employs many hands, becauſe often a thriftleſs heir ſuffers a house that his father built, to fall into decay, so that his successor must, at a great cost, repair that which he might have kept up with a small charge: and often it falls out, that the same house which one built at a vast expence, is neglected by another that thinks he has a more delicate sense of such things, and he suffering it to fall to ruin, builds another at no less charge. But among the Utopians, all things are so regulated, that men do very seldom build upon any new piece of ground; and they are not only very quick in repairing their houses, but shew their foresight in preventing their decay: so that their buildings are preserved very long, with very little labour: and thus the craftsmen to whom that care belongs, are often without any employment, except it be the hewing of timber, and the squaring of stones, that so the materials may be in readiness for raising a building very suddenly, when there is any occasion for it. As for their clothes, observe how little work goes for them: While they are at labour, they are clothed with leather and skins, cast carelessly about them, which will last seven years; and when they appear in public, they put on an upper garment, which hides the other: and these are all of one colour, and that is the natural colour of the wool: and as they need less woollen cloth than is used any where else, so that which they do need, is much less costly. They use linen cloth more; but that is prepared with less labour, and they value cloth only by the whiteness of the linen, or the cleanness of the wool, without much regard to the fineness of the thread; and whereas in other places, four or five upper garments of woollen cloth, and of different colours, and as many vests of silk will scarce serve one man; and those that are nicer, think ten too few; every man there is contented with one, which very oft serves him two years. Nor is there any thing that can tempt a man to desire more; for if he had them, he would neither be the warmer, nor would he make one jot the better appearance for it. And thus since they are all employed in some useful labour; and since they content themselves with fewer things, it falls out that there is a great abundance of all things among them: so that often, for want of other work, if there is any need of mending their high ways at any time, you will see marvellous numbers of people brought out to work at them; and when there is no occasion of any public work, the hours of working are lessened by public proclamation; for the magistrates do not engage the people into any needless labour, since by their constitution they aim chiefly at this, that except in so far as public necessity requires it, all the people may have as much free time for themselves as may be necessary for the improvement of their minds, for in this they think the happiness of life consists.

Of their Traffic.

BUT it is now time to explain to you the mutual intercourse of this people, their commerce, and the rules by which all things are distributed among them. As their cities are composed of families, so their families are made up of those that are nearly related to one another. Their women, when they grow up, are married out; but all the males, both children and grandchildren, live still in the same house, in great obedience to their common parent, unless age has weakned his understanding; and in that case, he that is next to him in age, comes in his room. But lest any city should become either out of measure great, or fall under a dispeopling by any accident, provision is made that none of their cities may have above six thousand families in it, besides those of the country round it; and that no family may have less than ten, and more than sixteen persons in it; but there can be no determined number for the children under age: and this rule is easily observed, by removing some of the children of a more fruitful couple, to any other family that does not abound so much in them. By the same rule, they supply cities that do not increase so fast, by others that breed faster: And if there is any increase over the whole island, then they draw out a number of their citizens out of the several towns, and send them over to the neighbouring continent; where, if they find that the inhabitants have more soil than they can well cultivate, they fix a colony, taking in the inhabitants to their society, if they will live with them; and where they do that of their own accord, they quickly go into their method of life, and to their rules, and this proves a happiness to both the nations: for according to their constitution, such care is taken of the soil, that it becomes fruitful enough for both, tho' it might be otherwise too narrow and barren for any one of them. But if the natives refuse to conform themselves to their laws, they drive them out of those bounds which they mark out for themselves, and use force if they resist. For they account it a very just cause of war, if any nation will hinder others to come and possess a part of their soil, of which they make no use, but let it lie idle and uncultivated; since every man has by the law of nature a right to such a waste portion of the earth, as is necessary for his subsistence. If any accident has so lessened the number of the inhabitants of any of their towns, that it cannot be made up from the other towns of the island, without diminishing them too much, which is said to have fallen out but twice, since they were first a people, by two plagues that were among them; then the number is filled up, by recalling so many out of their colonies, for they will abandon their colonies, rather than fuffer any of their towns to fink too low.

But to return to the manner of their living together; the antienteft of every family governs it, as has been faid. Wives ferve their hufbands, and children their parents, and always the younger ferves the elder. Every city is divided into four equal parts, and in the middle of every part there is a market-place: That which is brought thither manufactured by the feveral families, is carried from thence to houfes appointed for that purpofe, in which all things of a fort are laid by themfelves; and every father of a family goes thither, and takes whatfoever he or his family ftand in need of, without either paying for it, or laying in any thing in pawn or exchange for it. There is no reafon for denying any thing to any perfon, fince there is fuch plenty of every thing among them: and there is no danger of any man's afking more than he needs; for what fhould make any do that, fince they are all fure that they will be always fupplied? It is the fear of want that makes any of the whole race of animals, either greedy or ravenous; but befides fear, there is in man a vaft pride, that makes him fancy it a particular glory for him to excel others in pomp and excefs. But by the laws of the Utopians, there is no room for thefe things among them. Near thefe markets there are alfo others for all forts of victuals, where there are not only herbs, fruits and bread, but alfo fifh, fowl, and cattle. There are also without their towns, places appointed near some running water, for killing their beasts, and for washing away their filth; which is done by their slaves, for they suffer none of their citizens to kill their cattle, because they think, that pity and good nature, which are among the best of those affections that are born with us, are much impaired by the butchering of animals: Nor do they suffer any thing that is foul or unclean to be brought within their towns, left the air should be infected by ill smells which might prejudice their health. In every street there are great halls that lie at an equal distance from one another, which are marked by particular names. The syphogrants dwell in these; that are set over thirty families, fifteen lying on one side of it, and as many on the other. In these they do all meet and eat. The stewards of every one of them come to the market-place at an appointed hour; and according to the number of those that belong to their hall, they carry home provisions. But they take more care of their sick, than of any others, who are looked after and lodged in public hospitals: they have belonging to every town four hospitals, that are built without their walls, and are so large, that they may pass for little towns: by this means, if they had ever such a number of sick persons, they could lodge them conveniently, and at such a distance, that such of them as are sick of infectious diseases, may be kept so far from the rest, that there can be no danger of contagion. The hospitals are so furnished and stored with all things that are convenient for the ease and recovery of the sick; and those that are put in them, are all looked after with so tender and watchful a care, and are so constantly treated by their skilful physicians; that as none is sent to them against their will, so there is scarce one in a whole town, that if he should fall ill, would not choose rather to go thither, than lie sick at home.

After the steward of the hospitals has taken for them whatsoever the physician does prescribe at the market-place, then the best things that remain, are distributed equally among the halls, in proportion to their numbers, only, in the first place, they serve the prince, the chief priest, the tranibors and ambassadors, and strangers, (if there are any, which indeed falls out but seldom, and for whom there are houses well furnished, particularly appointed when they come among them.) At the hours of dinner and supper, the syphogranty being called together by sound of trumpet, meets and eats together, except only such as are in the hospitals, or lie sick at home. Yet after the halls are served, no man is hindered to carry provisions home from the market-place; for they know that none does that but for some good reason; for tho' any that will may eat at home, yet none does it willingly, since it is both an indecent and foolish thing, for any to give themselves the trouble to make ready an ill dinner at home, when there is a much more plentiful one made ready for him so near hand. All the uneasy and sordid services about these halls, are performed by their slaves; but the dressing and cooking their meat, and the ordering their tables, belongs only to the women, which goes round all the women of every family by turns. They sit at three or more tables, according to their numbers; the men sit towards the wall, and the women sit on the other side, that if any of them should fall suddenly ill, which is ordinary to women with child, she may, without disturbing the rest, rise and go to the nurses room, who are there with the suckling children; where there is always fire, and clean water at hand, and some cradles in which they may lay the young children, if there is occasion for it, and that they may shift and dress them before the fire. Every child is nursed by its own mother, if death or sickness does not intervene; and in that case the syphogrants wives find out a nurse quickly, which is no hard matter to do; for any one that can do it, offers herself chearfully: for as they are much inclined to that piece of mercy, so the child whom they nurse, considers the nurse as its mother. All the children under five years old, sit among the nurses, the rest of the younger sort of both sexes, till they are fit for marriage, do either serve those that sit at table; or if they are not strong enough for that, they stand by them in great silence, and eat that which is given them, by those that sit at table; nor have they any other formality of dining. In the middle of the firft table, which ftands in the upper end of the hall, a-crofs fits the fyphogrant and his wife, for that is the chief and moft confpicuous place: Next to him fit two of the moft ancient, for there go always four to a mefs. If there is a temple within that fyphogranty, the prieft and his wife fit with the fyphogrant above all the reft: Next them there is a mixture of old and young, who are fo placed, that as the young are fet near others, fo they are mixed with the more ancient, which they fay was appointed on this account, that the gravity of the old people, and the reverence that is due to them, might reftrain the younger from all indecent words and geftures. Difhes are not ferved up to the whole table at firft, but the beft are firft fet before the ancienter, whofe feats are diftinguifhed from the younger, and after them all the reft are ferved alike. The old men diftribute to the younger any curious meats that happen to be fet before them, if there is not fuch an abundance of them, that the whole company may be ferved by them.

Thus old men are honoured with a particular refpect; yet all the reft fare as well as they do. They begin both dinner and fupper with fome lecture of morality that is read to them; but it is fo fhort, that it is not tedious nor uneafy to them to hear it: Upon that the old men take occafion to entertain thofe about them, with fome ufeful and pleafant enlargements; but they do not engross the whole discourse so to themselves, during their meals, that the younger may not put in for a share: on the contrary, they engage them to talk, that so they may in that free way of conversation, find out the force of every one's spirit, and observe their temper. They dispatch their dinners quickly, but sit long at supper: because they go to work after the one, and are to sleep after the other, during which they think the stomach carries on the concoction more vigorously. They never sup without music; and there is always fruit served up after meat; while they sit at meat, some burn perfumes, and sprinkle about sweet ointments, and sweet waters: and they are wanting in nothing that may cheer up their spirits, for they give themselves a large allowance that way, and indulge themselves in all such pleasures as are attended with no inconvenience. Thus do those that are in the towns live together; but in the country, where they live at a greater distance, every one eats at home, and no family wants any necessary sort of provision, for it is from them that provisions are sent unto those that live in the towns.

Of the Travelling of the Utopians.

IF any of them has a mind to visit his friends that live in some other town, or desires to travel and see the rest of the country, he obtains leave very easily from the Syphogrant and Tranibors to do it, when there is no particular occasion for him at home: Such as travel, carry with them a passport from the Prince, which both certifies the licence that is granted for travelling, and limits the time of their return. They are furnished with a waggon and a slave, who drives the oxen, and looks after them: but unless there are women in the company, the waggon is sent back at the end of the journey as a needless trouble: While they are on the road, they carry no provisions with them; yet they want nothing, but are every way treated as if they were at home. If they stay in any place longer than a night, every one follows his proper occupation, and is very well used by those of his own trade: but if any man goes out of the city to which he belongs, without leave, and is found going about without a passport, he is roughly handled, and is punished as a fugitive, and sent home disgracefully; and if he falls again into the like fault, he is condemned to slavery. If any man has a mind to travel only over the precinct of his own city, he may freely do it, obtaining his father's permission, and his wife's consent; but when he comes into any of the country houses, he must labour with them according to their rules, if he expects to be entertained by them: and if he does this, he may freely go over the whole precinct, being thus as useful to the city to which he belongs, as if he were still within it. Thus you see that there are no idle persons among them, nor pretences of excusing any from labour. There are no taverns, no ale-houses, nor stews among them; nor any other occasions of corrupting themselves or of getting into corners or forming themselves into parties: all men live in full view, so that all are obliged, both to perform their ordinary task, and to employ themselves well in their spare hours. And it is certain, that a people thus ordered, must live in a great abundance of all things; and these being equally distributed among them, no man can want any thing, or be put to beg.

In their great council at Amaurot, to which there are three sent from every town once every year, they examine what towns abound in provisions, and what are under any scarcity, that so the one may be furnished from the other; and this is done freely, without any sort of exchange; for according to their plenty or scarcity, they supply, or are supplied from one another; so that indeed the whole island is, as it were, one family. When they have thus taken care of their whole country, and laid up stores for two years, which they do in cafe that an ill year fhould happen to come, then they order an exportation of the over-plus, both of corn, honey, wool, flax, wood, fcarlet, and purple; wax, tallow, leather, and cattle, which they fend out commonly in great quantities to other countries. They order a feventh part of all thefe goods to be freely given to the poor of the countries to which they fend them, and they fell the reft at moderate rates. And by this exchange, they not only bring back thofe few things that they need at home, for indeed they fcarce need any thing but iron, but likewife a great deal of gold and filver; and by their driving this trade fo long, it is not to be imagined how vaft a treafure they have got among them: fo that now they do not much care whether they fell off their merchandize for money in hand, or upon truft. A great part of their treafure is now in bonds; but in all their contracts no private man ftands bound, but the writing runs in name of the town; and the towns that owe them money, raife it from thofe private hands that owe it to them, and lay it up in their public chamber, or enjoy the profit of it till the Utopians call for it; and they choofe rather to let the greateft part of it lie in their hands, who make advantage by it, than to call for it themfelves: but if they fee that any of their other neighbours ftand more in need of it, then they raife it, and lend it to them; or ufe it themfelves, if they are engaged in a war, which is the only occafion that they can have for all that treasure that they have laid up; that so either in great extremities, or sudden accidents, they may serve themselves by it; chiefly for hiring foreign soldiers, whom they more willingly expose to danger than their own people: they give them great pay, knowing well that this will work even on their enemies, and engage them either to betray their own side, or at least to desert it, or will set them on to mutual factions among themselves: for this end they have an incredible treasure; but they do not keep it as a treasure, but in such a manner as I am almost afraid to tell it, lest you think it so extravagant, that you can hardly believe it; which I have the more reason to apprehend from others, because if I had not seen it myself, I could not have been easily persuaded to have believed it upon any man's report.

It is certain, that all things appear so far incredible to us, as they differ from our own customs: but one who can judge aright, will not wonder to find, that since their other constitutions differ so much from ours, their value of gold and silver should be measured, not by our standard, but by one that is very different from it; for since they have no use of money among themselves, but keep it for an accident; that tho' as it may possibly fall out, it may have great intervals; they value it no farther than it deserves, or may be useful to them. So that it is plain, that they must prefer iron either to gold or silver: for men can no more live without iron, than without fire or water; but nature has marked out no use for the other metals, with which we may not very well difpenfe. The folly of man has enhanfed the value of gold and filver, becaufe of their fcarcity: whereas on the contrary they reafon, that nature, as an indulgent parent, has given us all the beft things very freely, and in great abundance, fuch as are water and earth, but has laid up and hid from us the things that are vain and ufelefs.

If thofe metals were laid up in any tower among them, it would give jealoufy of the prince and fenate, according to that foolifh miftruft into which the rabble is apt to fall, as if they intended to cheat the people, and make advantages to themfelves by it; or if they fhould work it into veffels, or any fort of plate, they fear that the people might grow too fond of it, and fo be unwilling to let the plate be run down, if a war made it neceffary to pay their foldiers with it: therefore to prevent all thefe inconveniences, they have fallen upon an expedient, which as it agrees with their other policy, fo is very different from ours, and will fcarce gain belief among us, who value gold fo much, and lay it up fo carefully: for whereas they eat and drink out of veffels of earth, or glafs, that tho' they look very pretty, yet are of very flight materials; they make their chamber pots and clofe-ftools of gold and filver; and that not only in their public halls, but in their private houfes: Of the fame metals they likewife make chains and fetters for their slaves; and as a badge of infamy, they hang an ear-ring of gold to some, and make others wear a chain or a coronet of gold; and thus they take care, by all manner of ways, that gold and silver may be of no esteem among them; and from hence it is, that whereas other nations part with their gold and their silver, as unwillingly as if one tore out their bowels, those of Utopia would look on their giving in all their gold or silver, when there were any use for it, but as the parting with a trifle, or as we would estimate the loss of a penny. They find pearls on their coast; and diamonds, and carbuncles on their rocks: they do not look after them, but if they find them by chance, they polish them, and with them they adorn their children, who are delighted with them, and glory in them during their childhood; but when they grow to years, and see that none but children use such baubles, they of their own accord, without being bid by their parents, lay them aside, and would be as much ashamed to use them afterwards, as children among us, when they come to years, are of their nuts, puppets, and other toys.

I never saw a clearer instance of the different impressions that different customs make on people, than I observed in the ambassadors of the Anemolians who came to Amaurot when I was there. And because they came to treat of affairs of great consequence, the deputies from several towns had met to wait for their coming. The ambaſſadors of the nations that lie near Utopia, knowing their cuſtoms, and that fine clothes are of no eſteem among them; that ſilk is deſpiſed, and gold is a badge of infamy, uſe to come very modeſtly clothed; but the Anemolians that lay more remote, and ſo had little commerce with them, when they underſtood that they were coarſly clothed, and all in the ſame manner, they took it for granted that they had none of thoſe fine things among them of which they made no uſe; and they being a vain-glorious, rather than a wiſe people, reſolved to ſet themſelves out with ſo much pomp, that they ſhould look like gods, and ſo ſtrike the eyes of the poor Utopians with their ſplendor. Thus three ambaſſadors made their entry with an hundred attendants, that were all clad in garments of different colours, and the greater part in ſilk; the ambaſſadors themſelves, who were of the nobility of their country, were in cloth of gold, and adorned with maſſy chains, ear-rings and rings of gold: their caps were covered with bracelets ſet full of pearls and other gems: in a word, they were ſet out with all thoſe things, that among the Utopians were either the badges of ſlavery, the marks of infamy, or children's rattles. It was not unpleaſant to ſee on the one ſide how they look'd big, when they compared their rich habits with the plain clothes of the Utopians, who were come out in great numbers to ſee them make their entry. And on the other ſide, to obſerve how much they were miſ-

taken in the impression which they hoped this pomp
would have made on them; it appeared so ridiculous
a shew to all that had never stirred out of their country, and so had not seen the customs of other nations;
that tho' they paid some reverence to those that were
the most meanly clad, as if they had been the ambassadors, yet when they saw the ambassadors themselves,
so full of gold chains they looked upon them as slaves,
made them no reverence at all. You might have seen
their children, who were grown up to that bigness,
that they had thrown away their jewels, call to their
mothers, and push them gently, and cry out, See that
great fool that wears pearls and gems, as if he were
yet a child. And their mothers answered them in
good earnest, Hold your peace, this is I believe, one
of the ambassadors fools. Others censured the fashion
of their chains, and observed that they were of no
use, for they were too slight to bind their slaves, who
could easily break them; and they saw them hang so
loose about them, that they reckoned they could easily
throw them away, and so get from them. But after
the ambassadors had staid a day among them, and saw
so vast a quantity of gold in their houses, which was
as much despised by them, as it was esteemed in other
nations, and that there was more gold and silver in
the chains and fetters of one slave, than all their ornaments amounted to, their plumes fell, and they were
ashamed of all that glory for which they had formerly

valued themselves, and so laid it aside: to which they were the more determined, when upon their engaging into some free discourse with the Utopians, they discovered their sense of such things, and their other customs. The Utopians wonder how any man should be so much taken with the glaring doubtful lustre of a jewel or stone, that can look up to a star, or to the sun himself; or how any should value himself, because his cloth is made of a finer thread: for how fine soever that thread may be, it was once no better than the fleece of a sheep, and that sheep was a sheep still for all its wearing it. They wonder much to hear, that gold which in itself is so useless a thing, should be every where so much esteemed, that even man for whom it was made, and by whom it has its value, should yet be thought of less value than it is: so that a man of lead, who has no more sense than a log of wood, and is as bad as he is foolish, should have many wise and good men serving him, only because he has a great heap of that metal; and if it should so happen, that by some accident, or trick of law, which does sometimes produce as great changes as chance itself, all this wealth should pass from the master to the meanest varlet of his whole family, he himself would very soon become one of his servants, as if he were a thing that belonged to his wealth, and so were bound to follow its fortune. But they do much more admire and detest their folly, who when they see a rich man, tho' they neither owe him any thing, nor are in any fort obnoxious to him, yet merely becaufe he is rich, they give him little lefs than divine honours; even tho' they know him to be fo covetous and bafe minded, that notwithſtanding all his wealth, he will not part with one farthing of it to them as long as he lives.

 Thefe and fuch like notions has that people drunk in, partly from their education, being bred in a country, whofe cuſtoms and conftitutions are very oppofite to all fuch foolifh maxims: and partly from their learning and ſtudies: for tho' there are but few in any town that are excufed from labour, fo that they may give themfelves wholly to their ſtudies, thefe being only fuch perfons as difcover from their childhood an extraordinary capacity and difpofition for letters, yet their children and a great part of the nation, both men and women, are taught to fpend thofe hours in which they are not obliged to work, in reading: and this they do their whole life long. They have all their learning in their own tongue; which is both a copious and pleafant language, and in which a man can fully exprefs his mind: it runs over a great tract of many countries, but it is not equally pure in all places: they have never fo much as heard of the names of any of thofe philofophers that are fo famous in thefe parts of the world, before we went among them; and yet they had made the fame difcoveries that the Greeks had done, both in mufic, logic, arithmetic, and geometry. But as they are equal to the antient philosophers almost in all things, so they far exceed our modern logicians, for they have never yet fallen upon the barbarous niceties that our youth are forced to learn in those trifling logical schools that are among us; and they are so far from minding chimera's, and fantastical images made in the mind, that none of them could comprehend what we meant, when we talked to them of a man in the abstract, as common to all men in particular, (so that tho' we spoke of him as a thing that we could point at with our fingers, yet none of them could perceive him) and yet distinct from every one, as if he were some monstrous colossus or giant. Yet for all this ignorance of these empty notions, they knew astronomy, and all the motions of the orbs exactly; and they have many instruments, well contrived and divided, by which they do very accurately compute the course and positions of the sun, moon, and stars. But for the cheat, of divining by the stars, and by their oppositions or conjunctions, it has not so much as entred into their thoughts. They have a particular sagacity, founded on much observation, of judging of the weather, by which they know when they may look for rain, wind, or other alterations in the air: But as to the philosophy of those things, and the causes of the saltness of the sea, and of its ebbing and flowing, and of the original and nature both of the heavens and the earth; they dispute of them, partly, as our antient philosophers have done;

and, partly, upon some new hypothesis, in which, as they differ from them, so they do not in all things agree among themselves.

As for moral philosophy, they have the same disputes among them, that we have here: they examine what things are properly good, both for the body and the mind: and whether any outward thing can be called truly good, or if that term belongs only to the endowments of the mind. They inquire likewise into the nature of virtue and pleasure; but their chief dispute is, concerning the happiness of a man, and wherein it consists? Whether in some one thing, or in a great many? They seem indeed more inclinable to that opinion that places, if not the whole, yet the chief part of a man's happiness in pleasure; and which may seem more strange, they make use of arguments even from religion, notwithstanding its severity and roughness, for the support of that opinion, that is so indulgent to pleasure; for they never dispute concerning happiness without fetching some arguments from the principles of religion, as well as from natural reason; since without the former, they reckon that all our inquiries after happiness, must be but conjectural and defective.

Those principle of their religion, are, that the soul of man is immortal, and that God of his goodness has designed that it should be happy; and that he has therefore appointed rewards for good and virtuous actions, and punishments for vice, to be distributed after this life: And though thefe principles of religion are conveyed down among them by tradition, they think, that even reafon itfelf determines a man to believe and acknowledge them: and they freely confefs, that if thefe were taken away, no man would be fo infenfible, as not to feek after pleafure by all manner of ways, lawful or unlawful; ufing only this caution, that a leffer pleafure might not ftand in the way of a greater, and that no pleafure ought to be purfued, that fhould draw a great deal of pain after it: for they think it the maddeft thing in the world to purfue virtue, that is a four and difficult thing: and not only to renounce the pleafures of life, but willingly to undergo much pain and trouble, if a man has no profpect of a reward. And what reward can there be, for one that has paffed his whole life, not only without pleafure, but in pain, if there is nothing to be expected after death? Yet they do not place happinefs in all forts of pleafures, but only in thofe that in themfelves are good and honeft: for whereas there is a party among them that places happinefs in bare virtue, others think that our natures are conducted by virtue to happinefs, as that which is the chief good of man. They define virtue thus, that it is a living according to nature; and think that we are made by God for that end: they do believe that a man does then follow the dictates of nature, when he purfues or avoids things according to the direction of reafon: they fay, that the firft dictate of reason is, the kindling in us a love and reverence for the Divine Majesty, to whom we owe both all that we have, and all that we can ever hope for. In the next place, reason directs us, to keep our minds as free of passion, and as chearful as we can; and that we should consider ourselves as bound by the ties of good nature and humanity, to use our utmost endeavours to help forward the happiness of all other persons; for there was never any man that was such a morose and severe pursuer of virtue, and such an enemy to pleasure, that though he set hard rules to men to undergo, much pain, many watchings, and other rigours, yet did not at the same time advise them to do all they could in order to the relieving and easing such people as were miserable; and did not represent it as a mark of a laudable temper, that it was gentle and good natured: and they infer from thence, that if a man ought to advance the welfare and comfort of the rest of mankind, there being no virtue more proper and peculiar to our nature, than to ease the miseries of others, to free them from trouble and anxiety, in furnishing them with the comforts of life, that consist in pleasure; nature does much more vigorously lead him to do all this for himself. A life of pleasure, is either a real evil: and in that case we ought not only, not to assist others in their pursuit of it, but on the contrary, to keep them from it all we can, as from that which is hurtful and deadly to them; or if it is a good thing, so that we not only may, but ought to help others to it, why then ought not a man to begin with himſelf? Since no man can be more bound to look after the good of another, than after his own: for nature cannot direct us to be good and kind to others, and yet at the ſame time to be unmerciful and cruel to ourſelves. Thus as they define virtue to be a living according to nature, ſo they reckon that nature ſets all people on to ſeek after pleaſure, as the end of all they do. They do alſo obſerve, that in order to the ſupporting the pleaſures of life, nature inclines us to enter into ſociety; for there is no man ſo much raiſed above the reſt of mankind, that he ſhould be the only favourite of nature, which on the contrary ſeems to have levelled all thoſe together that belong to the ſame ſpecies. Upon this they infer, that no man ought to ſeek his own conveniences ſo eagerly, that thereby he ſhould prejudice others; and therefore they think, that not only all agreements between private perſons ought to be obſerved; but likewiſe, that all thoſe laws ought to be kept, which either a good prince has publiſhed in due form, or to which a people, that is neither oppreſſed with tyranny, nor circumvented by fraud, has conſented, for diſtributing thoſe conveniences of life which afford us all our pleaſures.

They think it is an evidence of true wiſdom, for a man to purſue his own advantages, as far as the laws allow it. They account it piety, to prefer the public good to one's private concerns; but they think it unjust, for a man to seek for his own pleasure, by snatching another man's pleasures from him. And on the contrary, they think it a sign of a gentle and good soul, for a man to dispense with his own advantage for the good of others; and that by so doing, a good man finds as much pleasure one way, as he parts with another; for as he may expect the like from others when he may come to need it, so if that should fail him, yet the sense of a good action, and the reflections that one makes on the love and gratitude of those whom he has so obliged, gives the mind more pleasure, than the body could have found in that from which it had restrained itself: they are also persuaded that God will make up the loss of those small pleasures, with a vast and endless joy, of which religion does easily convince a good soul.

Thus upon an inquiry into the whole matter, they reckon that all our actions, and even all our virtues terminate in pleasure, as in our chief end and greatest happiness; and they call every motion or state, either of body or mind, in which nature teaches us to delight, a pleasure. And thus they cautiously limit pleasure, only to those appetites to which nature leads us; for they reckon that nature leads us only to those delights to which reason as well as sense carries us, and by which we neither injure any other person, nor let go greater pleasures for it; and which do not draw troubles on us after them: but they look upon those delights which men, by a foolish tho' common mistake, call pleasure, as if they could change the nature of things, as well as the use of words, as things that not only do not advance our happiness, but do rather obstruct it very much, because they do so intirely possess the minds of those that once go into them, with a false notion of pleasure, that there is no room left for truer and purer pleasures.

There are many things that in themselves have nothing that is truly delighting: On the contrary, they have a good deal of bitterness in them; and yet by our perverse appetites after forbidden objects, are not only ranked among the pleasures, but are made even the greatest designs of life. Among those who pursue these sophisticated pleasures, they reckon those whom I mentioned before, who think themselves really the better for having fine clothes: in which they think they are doubly mistaken, both in the opinion that they have of their clothes, and in the opinion that they have of themselves; for if you consider the use of clothes, why should a fine thread be thought better than a coarse one? And yet that sort of men, as if they had some real advantages beyond others, and did not owe it wholly to their mistakes, look big, and seem to fancy themselves to be the more valuable on that account, and imagine that a respect is due to them for the sake of a rich garment, to which they would not have pretended, if they had been more meanly clothed; and they resent it as an affront, if that respect is not paid them. It is also a great folly to be taken with these outward marks of respect, which signify nothing: for what true or real pleasure can one find in this, that another man stands bare, or makes legs to him? Will the bending another man's thighs give you any ease? And will his head's being bare, cure the madness of yours? And yet it is wonderful to see how this false notion of pleasure bewitches many, who delight themselves with the fancy of their nobility, and are pleased with this conceit, that they are descended from ancestors, who have been held for some successions rich, and that they have had great possessions; for this is all that makes nobility at present; yet they do not think themselves a whit the less noble, tho' their immediate parents have left none of this wealth to them; or tho' they themselves have squandred it all away. The Utopians have no better opinion of those, who are much taken with gems and precious stones, and who account it a degree of happiness, next to a divine one, if they can purchase one that is very extraordinary; especially if it be of that sort of stones, that is then in greatest request: for the same sort is not at all times of the same value with all sorts of people; nor will men buy it, unless it be dismounted and taken out of the gold; and then the jeweller is made to give good security, and required solemnly to swear that the stone is true, that by such an exact caution, a false one may not be bought instead of a true: Whereas if you were to examine it, your eye could find no difference between that which is counterfeit, and that which is true; so that they are all one to you as much as if you were blind: And can it be thought that they who heap up an useless mass of wealth, not for any use that it is to bring them, but merely to please themselves with the contemplation of it, enjoy any true pleasure in it? The delight they find, is only a false shadow of joy: Those are no better, whose error is somewhat different from the former, and who hide it, out of their fear of losing it; for what other name can fit the hiding it in the earth, or rather the restoring it to it again, it being thus cut off from being useful, either to its owner, or to the rest of mankind? And yet the owner having hid it carefully, is glad, because he thinks he is now sure of it. And in case one should come to steal it, the owner, tho' he might live perhaps ten years after that, would all that while after the theft, of which he knew nothing, find no difference between his having it, or losing it, for both ways it was equally useless to him.

Among those foolish pursuers of pleasure, they reckon all those that delight in hunting, or birding, or gaming: of whose madness they have only heard, for they have no such things among them: But they have asked us, What sort of pleasure is it that men can find in throwing the dice? For if there were any pleasure in it, they think the doing it so often should give one a surfeit of it: And what pleasure can one find in hearing the barking and howling of dogs, which seem rather odious than pleasant sounds? Nor can they comprehend the pleasure of seeing dogs run after a hare, more than of seeing one dog run after another; for you have the same entertainment to the eye on both these occasions; if the seeing them run is that which gives the pleasure, since that is the same in both cases: but if the pleasure lies in seeing the hare killed and torn by the dogs, this ought rather to stir pity, when a weak, harmless and fearful hare, is devoured by a strong, fierce, and cruel dog. Therefore all this business of hunting, is among the Utopians turned over to their butchers; and those are all slaves, as was formerly said: and they look on hunting, as one of the basest parts of a butcher's work: for they account it both more profitable, and more decent to kill those beasts that are more necessary and useful to mankind; whereas the killing and tearing of so small and miserable an animal, which a huntsman proposes to himself, can only attract him with the false shew of pleasure; for it is of so little use to him; they look on the desire of the bloodshed, even of beasts, as a mark of a mind that is already corrupted with cruelty, or that at least by the frequent returns of so brutal a pleasure, must degenerate into it.

Thus tho' the rabble of mankind looks upon these, and all other things of this kind, which are indeed innumerable, as pleasures; the Utopians on the contrary observing, that there is nothing in the nature of them that is truly pleasant, conclude that they are not to be reckoned among pleasures: for tho' these things may create some tickling in the senses, (which seems to be a true notion of pleasure) yet they reckon that this does not arise from the thing itself, but from a depraved custom, which may so vitiate a man's taste, that bitter things may pass for sweet; as women with child think pitch or tallow tastes sweeter than honey; but as a man's sense when corrupted, either by a disease, or some ill habit, does not change the nature of other things, so neither can it change the nature of pleasure.

They reckon up several sorts of these pleasures, which they call true ones: some belong to the body, and others to the mind. The pleasures of the mind lie in knowledge, and in that delight which the contemplation of truth carries with it; to which they add the joyful reflections on a well spent life, and the assured hopes of a future happiness. They divide the pleasures of the body into two sorts; the one is that which gives our senses some real delight, and is performed, either by the recruiting of nature, and supplying those parts on which the internal heat of life feeds; and that is done by eating or drinking: or when nature is eased of any surcharge that oppresses it, as when we empty our guts, beget children, or free any of the parts of our body from aches or heats by friction. There is another kind of this sort of pleasure, that neither gives us any thing that our bodies require, nor frees us from any thing with which we are overcharged; and yet it excites our senses by a secret unseen virtue, and by a generous impression, it so tickles and affects them, that it turns them inwardly upon themselves; and this is the pleasure begot by music. Another sort of bodily pleasure is that which consists in a quiet and good constitution of body, by which there is an entire healthiness spread over all the parts of the body, not allay'd with any disease. This, when it is free from all mixture of pain, gives an inward pleasure of itself, even tho' it should not be excited by any external and delighting object; and altho' this pleasure does not so vigorously affect the sense, nor act so strongly upon it; yet as it is the greatest of all pleasures, so almost all the Utopians reckon it the foundation and basis of all the other joys of life; since this alone makes one's state of life to be easy and desirable; and when this is wanting, a man is really capable of no other pleasure. They look upon indolence and freedom from pain, if it does not rise from a perfect health, to be a state of stupidity rather than of pleasure. There has been a controversy in this matter very narrowly canvassed among them; whether a firm and entire health could be called a pleasure, or not? Some have thought that there was no pleasure, but that which was excited by some sensible motion in the body. But this opinion has been long ago run down among them, so that now they do almost all agree in this, that health is the greatest of all bodily pleasures; and that as there is a pain in sickness, which is as opposite in its nature to pleasure, as sickness itself is to health, so they hold that health carries a pleasure along with it: and if any should say, that sickness is not really a pain, but that it only carries a pain along with it, they look upon that as a fetch of subtility, that does not much alter the matter. So they think it is all one, whether it be said, that health is in itself a pleasure, or that it begets a pleasure, as fire gives heat; so it be granted, that all those whose health is entire, have a true pleasure in it: and they reason thus, What is the pleasure of eating, but that a man's health which had been weakened, does, with the assistance of food, drive away hunger, and so recruiting itself, recovers its former vigour? And being thus refreshed, it finds a pleasure in that conflict: and if the conflict is pleasure, the victory must yet breed a greater pleasure, except we will fancy that it becomes stupid as soon as it has obtained that which it pursued, and so does neither know nor rejoice in its own welfare. If it is said, that health cannot be felt, they absolutely deny that, for what man is in health, that does not perceive it when he is awake? Is there any man that is so dull and stupid, as not to acknowledge that he feels a delight in health? And what is delight, but another name for pleasure?

But of all pleasures, they esteem those to be the most valuable that lie in the mind; and the chief of these, are those that arise out of true virtue, and the witness of a good conscience: they account health the chief pleasure that belongs to the body; for they think that the pleasure of eating and drinking, and all the other delights of the body, are only so far desirable, as they give or maintain health: but they are not pleasant in themselves, otherwise than as they resist those impressions that our natural infirmity is still making upon us: and as a wise man desires rather to avoid diseases, than to take physic; and to be freed from pain, rather than to find ease by remedies: so it were a more desirable state, not to need this sort of pleasure, than to be obliged to indulge it. And if any man imagines that there is a real happiness in this pleasure, he must then confess that he would be the happiest of all men, if he were to lead his life in a perpetual hunger, thirst, and itching, and by consequence in perpetual eating, drinking, and scratching himself, which any one may easily see would be not only a base but a miserable state of life. These are indeed the lowest of pleasures, and the least pure: for we can never relish them, but when they are mixed with the contrary pains. The pain of hunger must give us the pleasure of eating; and here the pain out-ballances the pleasure: and as the pain is more vehement, so it lasts much longer; for as it is upon us before the pleasure comes, so it does not cease, but with the pleasure that extinguishes it, and that goes off with it: so that they think none of those pleasures are to be valued, but as they are necessary. Yet they rejoice in them, and with due gratitude acknowledge the tenderness of the great Author of nature, who has planted in us appetites, by which those things that are necessary for our preservation, are likewise made pleasant to us. For how miserable a thing would life be, if those daily diseases of hunger and thirst, were to be carried off by such bitter drugs, as we must use for those diseases that return seldomer upon us? And thus these pleasant, as well as proper gifts of nature, do maintain the strength and the sprightliness of our bodies.

They do also entertain themselves with the other delights that they let in at their eyes, their ears, and their nostrils, as the pleasant relishes and seasonings of life, which nature seems to have marked out peculiarly for man: since no other sort of animals contemplates the figure and beauty of the universe; nor is delighted with smells, but as they distinguish meats by them; nor do they apprehend the concords or discords of sounds; yet in all pleasures whatsoever, they observe this temper, that a lesser joy may not hinder a greater, and that pleasure may never breed pain, which they think does always follow dishonest pleasures. But they think it a madness for a man to wear out the beauty of his face, or the force of his natural strength, and to corrupt the sprightliness of his body by sloth and laziness, or to waste his body by fasting, and so to weaken the strength of his conſtitution, and reject the other delights of life; unleſs by renouncing his own ſatisfaction, he can either ſerve the public, or promote the happineſs of others, for which he expects a greater recompence from God. So that they look on ſuch a courſe of life, as a mark of a mind, that is both cruel to itſelf, and ingrateful to the Author of nature, as if we would not be beholden to him for his favours, and therefore would reject all his bleſſings, and ſhould afflict himſelf for the empty ſhadow of virtue; or for no better end, than to render himſelf capable to bear thoſe misfortunes which poſſibly will never happen.

This is their notion of virtue and of pleaſure; they think that no man's reaſon can carry him to a truer idea of them, unleſs ſome diſcovery from heaven ſhould inſpire one with ſublimer notions. I have not now the leiſure to examine all this, whether they think right or wrong in this matter: Nor do I judge it neceſſary, for I have only undertaken to give you an account of their conſtitution, but not to defend every thing that is among them. I am ſure, that whatſoever may be ſaid of their notions, there is not in the whole world, either a better people, or a happier government: their bodies are vigorous and lively; and though they are but of a middle ſtature, and though they have neither the fruitfulleſt ſoil, nor the pureſt air in the world; yet they do ſo fortify themſelves by their temperate courſe of life, againſt the unhealthineſs of their air; and by their industry they do so cultivate their soil, that there is no where to be seen a greater increase, both of corn and cattle, nor are there any where healthier men to be found, and freer from diseases than among them: for one may see there, not only such things put in practice, that husbandmen do commonly for manuring and improving an ill soil, but in some places a whole wood is plucked up by the roots, as well as whole ones planted in other places, where there were formerly none: In doing of this, the chief consideration they have is of carriage, that their timber may be either near their towns, or lie upon the sea, or some rivers, so that it may be floated to them; for it is a harder work to carry wood at any distance over land, than corn. The people are industrious, apt to learn, as well as chearful and pleasant; and none can endure more labour, when it is necessary, than they; but, except in that case, they love their ease. They are unwearied pursuers of knowledge; for when we had given them some hints of the learning and discipline of the Greeks, concerning whom we only instructed them, (for we know that there was nothing among the Romans, except their historians and their poets, that they would value much) it was strange to see how eagerly they were set on learning that language: We began to read a little of it to them, rather in compliance with their importunity, than out of any hopes of their profiting much by it: but after a very short trial, we found they made such a progress in it, that we saw our labour was like to be more successful than we could have expected. They learned to write their characters, and to pronounce their language so right, and took up all so quick, they remembred it so faithfully, and became so ready and correct in the use of it, that it would have looked like a miracle, if the greater part of those whom we taught had not been men, both of extraordinary capacity, and of a fit age for it: they were for the greatest part chosen out among their learned men, by their chief council, tho' some learned it of their own accord. In three years time they became masters of the whole language, so that they read the best of the Greek authors very exactly. I am indeed apt to think, that they learned that language the more easily, because it seems to be of kin to their own: I believe that they were a colony of the Greeks; for tho' their language comes nearer the Persian, yet they retain many names, both for their towns and magistrates, that are of Greek origination. I had happened to carry a great many books with me, instead of merchandise, when I sailed my fourth voyage; for I was so far from thinking of coming back soon, that I rather thought never to have returned at all, and I gave them all my books, among which many of Plato's and some of Aristotle's works were. I had also Theophrastus of plants, which to my great regret, was imperfect; for having laid it carelesly by, while we were at sea, a monkey had fallen upon it and had torn out leaves in many places. They have no books of grammar, but Lascares, for I did not carry Theodorus with me; nor have they any dictionaries but Hesychius and Dioscorides. They esteem Plutarch highly, and were much taken with Lucian's wit, and with his pleasant way of writing. As for the poets, they have Aristophanes, Homer, Euripides, and Sophocles of Aldus's edition; and for historians, they have Thucydides, Herodotus, and Herodian. One of my companions, Thricius Apinatus, happened to carry with him some of Hippocrates's works, and Galen's Microtechne, which they hold in great estimation; for tho' there is no nation in the world, that needs physic so little as they do, yet there is not any that honours it so much: they reckon the knowledge of it to be one of the pleasantest and profitablest parts of philosophy, by which, as they search into the secrets of nature, so they not only find marvellous pleasure in it, but think that in making such inquiries, they do a most acceptable thing to the Author of nature; and imagine that he, as all inventors of curious engines, has exposed to our view this great machine of the universe, we being the only creatures capable of contemplating it: and that therefore an exact and curious observer and admirer of his workmanship, is much more acceptable to him, than one of the herd; who as if he were a beast, and not capable of reason, looks on all this glorious scene, only as a dull and unconcerned spectator.

The minds of the Utopians, when they are once excited by learning, are very ingenious in finding out all such arts as tend to the conveniences of life. Two things they owe to us, which are the art of printing, and the manufacture of paper: yet they do not owe these so entirely to us, but that a great part of the invention was their own; for after we had shewed them some paper books of Aldus's impression, and began to explain to them the way of making paper, and of printing, tho' we spake but very crudely of both these, not being practised in either of them, they presently took up the whole matter from the hints that we gave them: and whereas before they only writ on parchment, or on the barks of trees, or reeds; they have now set up the manufacture of paper, and printing-presses: and tho' at first they could not arrive at a perfection in them, yet by making many essays, they at last found out, and corrected all their errors, and brought the whole thing to perfection; so that if they had but a good number of Greek authors, they would be quickly supplied with many copies of them: at present, tho' they have no more than those I have mentioned, yet by several impressions, they have multiplied them into many thousands. If any man should go among them, that had some extraordinary talent, or that by much travelling had observed the customs of many nations, (which made us to be so well received) he would be very welcome to them; for they are very desirous to know the state of the whole world. Very few go among them on the account of traffic, for what can a man carry to them but iron, or gold, or silver, which merchants desire rather to export, than import to any strange country: and as for their exportation, they think it better to manage that themselves, than to let foreigners come and deal in it, for by this means, as they understand the state of the neighbouring countries better, so they keep up the art of navigation, which cannot be maintained but by much practice in it.

Of their Slaves, and of their Marriages.

THEY do not make slaves of prisoners of war, except those that are taken fighting against them; nor of the sons of their slaves, nor of the slaves of other nations: The slaves among them, are only such as are condemned to that state of life for some crime that they had committed, or, which is more common, such as their merchants find condemned to die in those parts to which they trade, whom they redeem sometimes at low rates; and in other places they have them for nothing; and so they fetch them away. All their slaves are kept at perpetual labour, and are always chained, but with this difference, that they treat their own natives much worfe, looking on them as a more profligate fort of people; who not being reftrained from crimes, by the advantages of fo excellent an education, are judged worthy of harder ufage than others. Another fort of flaves, is, when fome of the poorer fort in the neighbouring countries, offer of their own accord to come and ferve them; they treat thefe better, and ufe them in all other refpects, as well as their own countrymen, except that they impofe more labour upon them, which is no hard tafk to them that have been accuftomed to it; and if any of thefe have a mind to go back to their own country, which indeed falls out but feldom, as they do not force them to ftay, fo they do not fend them away empty-handed.

I have already told you with what care they look after their fick, fo that nothing is left undone that can contribute either to their eafe or health: and for thofe who are taken with fixed and incurable difeafes, they ufe all poffible ways to cherifh them, and to make their lives as comfortable as may be: they vifit them often, and take great pains to make their time pafs off eafily: But when any is taken with a torturing and lingring pain, fo that there is no hope, either of recovery or eafe, the priefts and magiftrates come and exhort them, that fince they are now unable to go on with the bufinefs of life, and are become a burden to themfelves, and to all about them, fo that they have really outlived themfelves, they would no longer nourifh fuch a rooted diftemper, but would chufe rather to die, fince they cannot live, but in much mifery; being affured, that if they either deliver themfelves from their prifon and torture, or are willing that others fhould do it, they fhall be happy after their deaths: and fince by their dying thus, they lofe none of the pleafures, but only the troubles of life; they think they act, not only reafonably in fo doing, but religioufly and pioufly; becaufe they follow the advices that are given them by the priefts, who are the expounders of the will of God to them. Such as are wrought on by thefe perfuafions, do either ftarve themfelves of their own accord, or they take opium, and fo they die without pain. But no man is forced on this way of ending his life; and if they cannot be perfuaded to it, they do not for that fail in their attendance and care of them: But as they believe that a voluntary death, when it is chofen upon fuch an authority, is very honourable; fo if any man takes away his own life, without the approbation of the priefts and the fenate, they give him none of the honours of a decent funeral, but throw his body into fome ditch.

Their women are not married before eighteen, nor their men before two and twenty; and if any of them run into forbidden embraces before their marriage, they are feverely punifhed, and the privilege of marriage is denied them, unlefs there is a fpecial warrant obtained for it afterward from the prince. Such diforders cast a great reproach upon the master and mistress of the family in which they fall out; for it is supposed, that they have been wanting to their duty. The reason of punishing this so severely, is, because they think that if they were not strictly restrained from all vagrant appetites, very few would engage in a married state, in which men venture the quiet of their whole life, being restricted to one person; besides many other inconveniences that do accompany it. In the way of choosing of their wives, they use a method that would appear to us very absurd and ridiculous, but is constantly observed among them, and accounted a wise and good rule. Before marriage, some grave matron presents the bride naked, whether she is a virgin or a widow, to the bridegroom; and after that, some grave man presents the bridegroom naked to the bride. We indeed both laughed at this, and condemned it as a very indecent thing. But they, on the other hand, wondred at the folly of the men of all other nations; who if they are but to buy a horse of a small value, are so cautious, that they will see every part of him, and take off both his saddle, and all his other tackle, that there may be no secret ulcer hid under any of them; and that yet in the choice of a wife, on which depends the happiness or unhappiness of the rest of his life, a man should venture upon trust, and only see about an handbreadth of the face, all the rest of the body being covered; under which there may lie hid that which may be contagious, as well as loathsome. All men are not so wise, that they chuse a woman only for her good qualities; and even wise men consider the body, as that which adds not a little to the mind: and it is certain, there may be some such deformity covered with one's clothes, as may totally alienate a man from his wife, when it is too late to part with her: for if such a thing is discovered after marriage, a man has no remedy but patience: so they think it is reasonable, that there should be a good provision made against such mischievous frauds.

There was so much the more reason in making a regulation in this matter, because they are the only people of those parts that do neither allow of polygamy, nor of divorces, except in the cases of adultery, or insufferable perverseness: for in these cases the senate dissolves the marriage, and grants the injured person leave to marry again; but the guilty are made infamous, and are never allowed the privilege of a second marriage. None are suffered to put away their wives against their wills, because of any great calamity that may have fallen on their person; for they look on it as the height of cruelty and treachery to abandon either of the married persons, when they need most the tender care of their consort; and that chiefly in the case of old age, which as it carries many diseases along with it, so it is a disease of itself. But it falls often out, that when a married couple do not agree well together, they by mutual confent feparate, and find out other perfons with whom they hope they may live more happily: Yet this is not done, without obtaining leave of the fenate; which never admits of a divorce, but upon a ftrict inquiry made, both by the fenators and their wives, into the grounds upon which it proceeds: and even when they are fatisfied concerning the reafons of it, they go on but flowly, for they reckon that too great eafinefs, in granting leave for new marriages, would very much fhake the kindnefs of married perfons. They punifh feverely thofe that defile the marriage bed: If both parties are married, they are divorced, and the injured perfons may marry one another, or whom they pleafe; but the adulterer and the adulterefs are condemned to flavery. Yet if either of the injured perfons cannot fhake off the love of the married perfon, they may live with them ftill in that ftate; but they muft follow them to that labour to which the flaves are condemned; and fometimes the repentance of the condemned perfon, together with the unfhaken kindnefs of the innocent and injured perfon, has prevailed fo far with the prince, that he has taken off the fentence: But thofe that relapfe, after they are once pardoned, are punifhed with death.

Their law does not determine the punifhment for other crimes; but that is left to the fenate, to temper it according to the circumftances of the fact. Hufbands have power to correct their wives, and parents to correct their children, unless the fault is so great, that a public punishment is thought necessary for the striking terror into others. For the most part, slavery is the punishment even of the greatest crimes; for as that is no less terrible to the criminals themselves than death; so they think the preserving them in a state of servitude, is more for the interest of the common-wealth, than the killing them outright; since as their labour is a greater benefit to the public, than their death could be, so the sight of their misery is a more lasting terror to other men, than that which would be given by their death. If their slaves rebel, and will not bear their yoke, and submit to the labour that is enjoined them, they are treated as wild beasts that cannot be kept in order, neither by a prison, nor by their chains; and are at last put to death. But those who bear their punishment patiently, and are so much wrought on by that pressure, that lies so hard on them, that it appears that they are really more troubled for the crimes they have committed, than for the miseries they suffer, are not out of hope, but that at last either the prince will, by his prerogative, or the people will by their intercession restore them again to their liberty, or at least very much mitigate their slavery. He that tempts a married woman to adultery, is no less severely punished, than he that commits it; for they reckon that a laid and studied design of committing any crime, is equal to the fact itself; since its not taking effect does not make the person that did all that in him lay in order to it, a whit the less guilty.

They take great pleasure in fools, and as it is thought a base and unbecoming thing to use them ill, so they do not think it amiss for people to divert themselves with their folly: and they think this is a great advantage to the fools themselves: for if men were so sullen and severe, as not at all to please themselves with their ridiculous behaviour, and foolish sayings, which is all that they can do to recommend themselves to others, it could not be expected that they would be so well look'd to, nor so tenderly used as they must otherwise be. If any man should reproach another for his being misshaped or imperfect in any part of his body, it would not at all be thought a reflection on the person that were so treated, but it would be accounted a very unworthy thing for him that had upbraided another with that which he could not help. It is thought a sign of a sluggish and sordid mind, not to preserve carefully one's natural beauty; but it is likewise an infamous thing among them to use paint or fard. And they all see that no beauty recommends a wife so much to her husband, as the probity of her life, and her obedience: for as some few are catched and held only by beauty, so all people are held by the other excellencies which charm all the world.

As they fright men from committing crimes by punishments, so they invite them to the love of virtue, by public honours: therefore they erect statues in honour to the memories of such worthy men as have deserved well of their country, and set these in their market-places, both to perpetuate the remembrance of their actions, and to be an incitement to their posterity to follow their example.

If any man aspires to any office, he is sure never to compass it: they live all easily together, for none of the magistrates are either insolent or cruel to the people; but they affect rather to be called fathers, and by being really so, they well deserve that name; and the people pay them all the marks of honour the more freely, because none are exacted of them. The prince himself has no distinction, either of garments or of a crown; but is only known by a sheaf of corn that is carried before him, as the high priest is also known by a wax light that is carried before him.

They have but few laws, and such is their constitution, that they need not many. They do very much condemn other nations, whose laws, together with the commentaries on them, swell up to so many volumes; for they think it an unreasonable thing to oblige men to obey a body of laws, that are both of such a bulk, and so dark, that they cannot be read or understood by every one of the subjects.

They have no lawyers among them, for they consider them as a sort of people, whose profession it is to disguise matters, as well as to wrest laws; and therefore they think it is much better that every man should plead his own cause, and trust it to the judge, as well as in other places the client does it to a counsellor. By this means they both cut off many delays, and find out truth more certainly: for after the parties have laid open the merits of their cause, without those artifices which lawyers are apt to suggest, the judge examines the whole matter, and supports the simplicity of such well-meaning persons, whom otherwise crafty men would be sure to run down: and thus they avoid those evils, which appear very remarkably among all those nations that labour under a vast load of laws. Every one of them is skilled in their law, for as it is a very short study, so the plainest meaning of which words are capable, is always the sense of their laws. And they argue thus; all laws are promulgated for this end, that every man may know his duty; and therefore the plainest and most obvious sense of the words, is that which must be put on them; since a more refined exposition cannot be easily comprehended, and laws become thereby useless to the greater part of mankind, who need most the direction of them: for to them it is all one, not to make a law at all, and to couch it in such terms, that without a quick apprehension, and much study, a man cannot find out the true meaning of it; and the generality of mankind are both so dull, and so much employed in their several trades, that they have neither the leisure nor the capacity requisite for such an inquiry.

Some of their neighbours, who are masters of their own liberties, having long ago, by the assistance of the Utopians, shaken off the yoke of tyranny; and being much taken with those virtues that they observe among them, have come to them, and desired that they would send magistrates among them to govern them; some changing them every year, and others every five years. At the end of their government, they bring them back to Utopia, with great expressions of honour and esteem, and carry away others to govern in their stead. In this they seem to have fallen upon a very good expedient for their own happiness and safety: for since the good or ill condition of a nation depends so much upon their magistrates, they could not have made a better choice, than by pitching on men whom no advantages can bias; for wealth is of no use to them, since they must go so soon back to their own country; and they being strangers among them, are not engaged in any of their heats or animosities: and it is certain, that when public judicatories are swayed, either by partial affections, or by avarice, there must follow upon it a dissolution of all justice, which is the chief sinew of society.

The Utopians call those nations that come and ask magistrates from them, *neighbours;* but they call those to whom they have been more particularly assisting, *friends*. And whereas all other nations are perpetually either making leagues or breaking them, they never enter into any alliance with any other state. They think leagues are useless things, and reckon, that if the common ties of human nature do not knit men together, the faith of promises will have no great effect on them: And they are the more confirmed in this, by that which they see among the nations round about them, who are no strict observers of leagues and treaties. We know how religiously they are observed in Europe; more particularly where the Christian doctrine is received, among whom they are sacred and inviolable. Which is partly owing to the justice and goodness of the princes themselves, and partly to their reverence that they pay to the popes: who as they are most religious observers of their own promises, so they exhort all other princes to perform theirs; and when fainter methods do not prevail, they compel them to it by the severity of the pastoral censure; and think that it would be the most indecent thing possible, if men who are particularly designed by the title of *the Faithful*, should not religiously keep the *Faith* of their treaties. But in that new found world, which is not more distant from us in situation, than it is disagreeing from us in their manners and course of life, there is no trusting to leagues, even tho' they were made with all the pomp of the most sacred ceremonies that is possible: On the contrary, they are the sooner broken for that, some slight pretences being found in the words of the treaties, which are contrived in such ambiguous terms, and that on design, that they can never be so strictly bound, but they will always find some loop-hole to escape at; and so they break both their leagues and their faith. And this is done with that impudence, that those very men who value themselves on having suggested these advices to their princes, would yet, with a haughty scorn, declaim against such craft, or, to speak plainer, such fraud and deceit, if they found private men make use of it in their bargains; and would readily say, that they deserved to be hanged for it.

By this means it is, that all sort of justice passes in the world, but for a low-spirited and vulgar virtue, which is far below the dignity of royal greatness. Or at least, there are two sorts of justice set up: The one is mean, and creeps on the ground, and therefore becomes none but the baser sort of men, and so must be kept in severely by many restraints, that it may not break out beyond the bounds that are set to it. The other is the peculiar virtue of princes, which as it is more majestic than that which becomes the rabble, so takes a freer compass; and lawful or unlawful, are only measured by pleasure and interest. These practices among the princes that lie about Utopia, who make so little account of their faith, seem to be the reasons that determine them to engage in no confederacies: Perhaps they would change their mind if they lived among us: But yet though treaties were more religiously observed, they would still dislike the custom of making them; since the world has taken up a false maxim upon it; as if there were no tie of nature knitting one nation to another, that are only separated perhaps by a mountain, or a river, and that all were born in a state of hostility, and so might lawfully do all that mischief to their neighbours, against which there is no provision made by treaties: And that when treaties are made, they do not cut off the enmity, or restrain the licence of preying upon one another, if by the unskilfulness of wording them, there are not effectual proviso's made against them. They on the other hand judge, that no man is to be esteemed our enemy that has never injured us; and that the partnership of the human nature, that is among all men, is instead of a league. And that kindness and good nature unite men more effectually, and more forcibly than any agreements whatsoever; since thereby the engagements of men's hearts become stronger, than any thing can be to which a few words can bind them.

Of their Military Discipline.

THEY detest war as a very brutal thing; and which, to the reproach of human nature, is more practised by men, than by any sort of beasts: and they, against the cuftom of almoft all other nations, think that there is nothing more inglorious than that glory that is gained by war: and therefore tho' they accuftom themfelves daily to military exercifes, and the difcipline of war; in which not only their men, but their women likewife, are trained up, that fo in cafes of neceffity, they may not be quite ufelefs: yet they do not rafhly engage in war, unlefs it be either to defend themfelves, or their friends, from any unjuft aggreffors; or out of good nature; or in compaffion to an oppreffed nation, that they affift them to the fhaking off the yoke of tyranny. They indeed help their friends, not only in defenfive, but alfo in offenfive wars: but they never do that, unlefs they had been confulted with while the matter was yet entire; and that being fatisfied with the grounds on which they went; they had found that all demands of reparation were rejected, fo that a war was neceffary: which they do not think to be only juft, when one neighbour makes an inrode on another, by public order, and carries away their fpoils; but when the merchants of one country are oppreffed in another; either under the pretence of fome unjuft laws, or by the perverfe wrefting of good ones: This they count a jufter caufe of war than the other, becaufe thofe injuries are done under fome colour of laws. This was the only ground of that war, in which they engaged with the Nephelogetes againft the Aleopolitanes, a little before our time: for the merchants of the former, having, as they thought, met with great injuſtice among the latter, that whether it was in itſelf right or wrong, did draw on a terrible war, many of their neighbours being engaged in it; and their keenneſs in carrying it on, being ſupported by their ſtrength in maintaining it; it not only ſhook ſome very flouriſhing ſtates, and very much afflicted others; but after a ſeries of much miſchief, it ended in the intire conqueſt and ſlavery of the Aleopolitanes, who tho' before the war, they were in all reſpects much ſuperior to the Nephelogetes, yet by it they fell under their empire; but the Utopians, tho' they had aſſiſted them in the war, yet pretended to no ſhare of the ſpoil.

But tho' they aſſiſt their friends ſo vigorouſly, in taking reparations for injuries that are done them in ſuch matters; yet if they themſelves ſhould meet with any ſuch fraud, provided there were no violence done to their perſons, they would only carry it ſo far, that unleſs ſatisfaction were made, they would give over trading with ſuch a people. This is not done becauſe they conſider their neighbours more than their own citizens; but ſince their neighbours trade every one upon his own ſtock, fraud is a more ſenſible injury to them, than it is to the Utopians, among whom the public only ſuffers in ſuch a caſe: and ſince they expect nothing in return for the merchandiſe that they export, but that in which they abound ſo much, and is of little use to them, the loss does not much affect them; therefore they think it would be too severe a thing to revenge a loss that brings so little inconvenience with it, either to their life or to their livelihood, with the death of many people; but if any of their people is either killed or wounded wrongfully, whether that be done by public authority, or only by private men, as soon as they hear of it, they send ambassadors, and demand, that the guilty persons may be delivered up to them; and if that is denied, they declare war; but if that is done, they condemn those either to death or slavery.

They would be both troubled and ashamed of a bloody victory over their enemies; and think it would be as foolish a purchase, as to buy the most valuable goods at too high a rate. And in no victory do they glory so much, as in that which is gained by dexterity and good conduct, without bloodshed. They appoint public triumphs in such cases, and erect trophies to the honour of those who have succeeded well in them; for then do they reckon that a man acts suitably to his nature, when he conquers his enemy in such a way, that no other creature but a man could be capable of it, and that is, by the strength of his understanding. Bears, lions, boars, wolves and dogs, and other animals, employ their bodily force one against another, in which as many of them are superior to man, both in strength and fierceness, so they are all subdued by the reason and understanding that is in him.

The only design of the Utopians in war, is to obtain that by force, which if it had been granted them in time, would have prevented the war; or if that cannot be done, to take so severe a revenge of those that have injured them, that they may be terrified from doing the like in all time coming. By these ends they measure all their designs, and manage them so, that it is visible that the appetite of fame or vain-glory, does not work so much on them, as a just care of their own security.

As soon as they declare war, they take care to have a great many schedules, that are sealed with their common seal, affixed in the most conspicuous places of their enemies country. This is carried secretly, and done in many places all at once. In those they promise great rewards to such as shall kill the prince, and lesser in proportion to such as shall kill any other persons, who are those on whom, next to the prince himself, they cast the chief blame of the war. And they double the sum to him, that instead of killing the person so marked out, shall take him alive, and put him in their hands. They offer not only indemnity, but rewards, to such of the persons themselves that are so marked, if they will act against their countrymen. By this means those that are named in their schedules, become not only distrustful of their fellow-citizens, but are jealous of one another; and are much diſtracted by fear and danger; for it has often fallen out, that many of them, and even the prince himſelf, have been betrayed by thoſe in whom they have truſted moſt: for the rewards that the Utopians offer, are ſo unmeaſurably great, that there is no ſort of crime to which men cannot be drawn by them. They conſider the riſk that thoſe run, who undertake ſuch ſervices, and offer a recompence proportioned to the danger; not only a vaſt deal of gold, but great revenues in lands, that lie among other nations that are their friends, where they may go and enjoy them very ſecurely; and they obſerve the promiſes they make of this kind moſt religiouſly. They do very much approve of this way of corrupting their enemies, tho' it appears to others to be a baſe and cruel thing; but they look on it as a wiſe courſe, to make an end of that which would be otherwiſe a great war, without ſo much as hazarding one battle to decide it. They think it likewiſe an act of mercy and love to mankind, to prevent the great ſlaughter of thoſe that muſt otherwiſe be killed in the progreſs of the war, both of their own ſide, and of their enemies, by the death of a few that are moſt guilty; and that in ſo doing, they are kind even to their enemies, and pity them no leſs than their own people, as knowing that the greater part of them do not engage in the war of their own accord, but are driven into it by the paſſions of their prince.

If this method does not succeed with them, then they sow seeds of contention among their enemies, and animate the prince's brother, or some of the nobility, to aspire to the crown. If they cannot disunite them by domestic broils, then they engage their neighbours against them, and make them set on foot some old pretensions, which are never wanting to princes, when they have occasion for them. And they supply them plentifully with money, tho' but very sparingly with any auxiliary troops: for they are so tender of their own people, that they would not willingly exchange one of them, even with the prince of their enemies country.

But as they keep their gold and silver only for such an occasion, so when that offers itself, they easily part with it, since it would be no inconvenience to them, tho' they should reserve nothing of it to themselves. For besides the wealth that they have among them at home, they have a vast treasure abroad; many nations round about them, being deep in their debt: So that they hire soldiers from all places for carrying on their wars; but chiefly from the Zapoletes, who lie five hundred miles from Utopia eastward. They are a rude, wild, and fierce nation, who delight in the woods and rocks, among which they were born and bred up. They are hardned both against heat, cold, and labour, and know nothing of the delicacies of life. They do not apply themselves to agriculture, nor do they care either for their houses or their clothes. Cattle is all that they look after; and for the greatest part, they live either by their hunting, or upon rapine; and are made, as it were, only for war. They watch all opportunities of engaging in it, and very readily embrace such as are offered them. Great numbers of them will often go out, and offer themselves upon a very low pay, to serve any that will employ them: They know none of the arts of life, but those that lead to the taking it away; they serve those that hire them, both with much courage and great fidelity; but will not engage to serve for any determined time, and agree upon such terms, that the next day they may go over to the enemies of those whom they serve, if they offer them a greater pay: and they will perhaps return to them the day after that, upon a higher advance of their pay. There are few wars in which they make not a considerable part of the armies of both sides: So it falls often out, that they that are of kin to one another, and were hired in the same country, and so have lived long and familiarly together; yet they forgetting both their relation and former friendship, kill one another upon no other consideration, but because they are hired to it for a little money, by princes of different interests: And so great regard have they to money, that they are easily wrought on by the difference of one penny a day, to change sides. So entirely does their avarice turn them, and yet this money on which they are so much set, is of little use to them; for what they purchase thus with their blood, they quickly waste it on luxury, which among them is but of a poor and miserable form.

This nation serves the Utopians against all people whatsoever, for they pay higher than any other. The Utopians hold this for a maxim, that as they seek out the best sort of men for their own use at home, so they make use of this worst sort of men for the consumption of war; and therefore they hire them with the offers of vast rewards, to expose themselves to all sorts of hazards, out of which the greater part never returns to claim their promises. Yet they make them good most religiously to such as escape. And this animates them to adventure again, when there is occasion for it; for the Utopians are not at all troubled how many of them soever happen to be killed; and reckon it a service done to mankind, if they could be a mean to deliver the world from such a lewd and vicious sort of people, that seem to have run together, as to the drain of human nature. Next to these, they are served in their wars, with those upon whose account they undertake them, and with the auxiliary troops of their other friends, to whom they join some few of their own people, and send some man of eminent and approved virtue to command in chief. There are two sent with him, who during his command, are but private men; but the first is to succeed him if he should happen to ted into it by baptism. But as two of our number were dead, so none of the four that survived, were in priests orders; therefore we could do no more but baptize them; so that to our great regret, they could not partake of the other sacraments, that can only be administred by priests: but they are instructed concerning them, and long most vehemently for them; and they were disputing very much among themselves, whether one that were chosen by them to be a priest, would not be thereby qualified to do all the things that belong to that character, even tho' he had no authority derived from the Pope; and they seemed to be resolved to choose some for that employment, but they had not done it when I left them.

Those among them that have not received our religion, yet do not fright any from it, and use none ill that goes over to it; so that all the while I was there, one man was only punished on this occasion. He being newly baptized, did, notwithstanding all that we could say to the contrary, dispute publicly concerning the Christian religion, with more zeal than discretion; and with so much heat, that he not only prefer'd our worship to theirs, but condemned all their rites as profane; and cried out against all that adhered to them, as impious and sacrilegious persons, that were to be damned to everlasting burnings. Upon this he, having preached these things often, was seized on, and after a trial, he was condemned to banishment, not for having disparaged their religion, but for his inflaming the people to sedition: for this is one of their antientest laws, that no man ought to be punished for his religion. At the first constitution of their government, Utopus having understood, that before his coming among them, the old inhabitants had been engaged in great quarrels concerning religion, by which they were so broken among themselves, that he found it an easy thing to conquer them, since they did not unite their forces against him, but every different party in religion fought by themselves: upon that, after he had subdu'd them, he made a law that every man might be of what religion he pleased, and might endeavour to draw others to it by the force of argument, and by amicable and modest ways, but without bitterness against those of other opinions; but that he ought to use no other force but that of persuasion; and was neither to mix reproaches nor violence with it; and such as did otherwise were to be condemned to banishment or slavery.

This law was made by Utopus, not only for preserving the public peace, which he saw suffered much by daily contentions and irreconcilable heats in these matters, but because he thought the interest of religion itself required it. He judged it was not fit to determine any thing rashly in that matter; and seemed to doubt whether those different forms of religion might not all come from God, who might inspire men differently, he being possibly pleased with a variety in it: and so he thought it was a very indecent and foolish thing for any man to frighten and threaten other men to believe any thing because it seemed true to him; and in case that one religion were certainly true, and all the rest false, he reckoned that the native force of truth would break forth at last, and shine bright, if it were managed only by the strength of argument, and with a winning gentleness; whereas if such matters were carried on by violence and tumults, then, as the wickedest sort of men is alway the most obstinate, so the holiest and best religion in the world might be overlaid with so much foolish superstition, that it would be quite choaked with it, as corn is with briars and thorns; therefore he left men wholly to their liberty in this matter, that they might be free to believe as they should see cause; only he made a solemn and severe law against such as should so far degenerate from the dignity of human nature, as to think that our souls died with our bodies, or that the world was governed by chance, without a wise over-ruling providence: for they did all formerly believe that there was a state of rewards and punishments to the good and bad after this life; and they look on those that think otherwise, as scarce fit to be counted men, since they degrade so noble a being as our soul is, and reckon it to be no better than a beast's; so far are they from looking on such men as fit for human society, or to be citizens of a well-ordered commonwealth; since a man of such principles must needs, as oft as he dares do it, despise all their laws and customs: for there is no doubt to be made, that a man who is afraid of nothing but the law, and apprehends nothing after death, will not stand to break through all the laws of his country, either by fraud or force, that so he may satisfy his appetites. They never raise any that hold these maxims, either to honours or offices, nor employ them in any public trust, but despise them, as men of base and sordid minds: yet they do not punish them, because they lay this down for a ground, that a man cannot make himself believe any thing he pleases; nor do they drive any to dissemble their thoughts by threatnings, so that men are not tempted to lie or disguise their opinions among them; which being a sort of fraud, is abhorred by the Utopians: they take indeed care that they may not argue for these opinions, especially before the common people: but they do suffer, and even encourage them to dispute concerning them in private with their priests, and other grave men, being confident that they will be cured of those mad opinions, by having reason laid before them. There are many among them that run far to the other extreme, tho' it is neither thought an ill nor unreasonable opinion, and therefore is not at all discouraged. They think that the souls of beasts are immortal, tho' far inferior to the dignity of the human soul, and not capable of so great a happiness. They are almost all of them very firmly persuaded, that good men will be infinitely happy in another state; so that tho' they are compassionate to all that are sick, yet they lament no mans death, except they see him part with life uneasy, and as if he were forced to it; for they look on this as a very ill presage, as if the soul being conscious to itself of guilt, and quite hopless, were afraid to die, from some secret hints of approaching misery. They think that such a man's appearance before God, cannot be acceptable to him, who being called on, does not go out chearfully, but is backward and unwilling, and is, as it were, dragged to it. They are struck with horror, when they see any die in this manner, and carry them out in silence, and with sorrow, and praying God that he would be merciful to the errors of the departed soul, they lay the body in the ground: but when any die chearfully, and full of hope, they do not mourn for them, but sing hymns when they carry out their bodies, and commending their souls very earnestly to God, in such a manner, that their whole behaviour is rather grave than sad, they burn their body, and set up a pillar where the pile was made, with an inscription to the honour of such men's memory. And when they come from the funeral, they discourse of their good life, and worthy actions, but speak of nothing oftner and with more pleasure, than of their serenity at their death. They think such respect paid to the memory of good men, is both the greatest incitement to engage others to follow their example, and the most acceptable worship that can be offered them; for they believe, that tho', by the imperfection of human sight, they are invisible to us, yet they are present among us, and hear those discourses that pass concerning themselves. And they think that it does not agree to the happiness of departed souls, not to be at liberty to be where they will: nor do they imagine them capable of the ingratitude of not desiring to see those friends, with whom they lived on earth in the strictest bonds of love and kindness: and they judge, that such good principles, as all other good things, are rather increased than lessened in good men after their death: so that they conclude they are still among the living, and do observe all that is said or done by them. And they engage in all affairs that they set about, with so much the more assurance, trusting to their protection; and the opinion that they have of their ancestors being still present, is a great restraint on them from all ill designs.

They despise and laugh at all sorts of auguries, and the other vain and superstitious ways of divination, that are so much observed among other nations; but they have great reverence for such miracles as cannot flow from any of the powers of nature, and look on them as effects and indications of the presence of the supream being, of which they say many instances have occurred among them; and that sometimes their public prayers, which upon great and dangerous occasions they have solemnly put up to God, with assured confidence of being heard, have been anfwered in a miraculous manner.

They think the contemplating God in his works, and the adoring him for them, is a very acceptable piece of worfhip to him.

There are many among them, that upon a motive of religion, neglect learning, and apply themfelves to no fort of ftudy; nor do they allow themfelves any leifure-time, but are perpetually employed in doing fomewhat, believing that by the good things that a man does he fecures to himfelf that happinefs that comes after death. Some of thefe vifit the fick; others mend high-ways, cleanfe ditches, or repair bridges, and dig turf, gravel, or ftones. Others fell and cleave timber, and bring wood, corn, and other neceffaries, on carts into their towns. Nor do thefe only ferve the public, but they ferve even private men, more than the flaves themfelves do: for if there is any where a rough, hard, and fordid piece of work to be done, from which many are frightened by the labour and loathfomenefs of it, if not the defpair of accomplifhing it, they do chearfully, and of their own accord, take that to their fhare; and by that means, as they eafe others very much, fo they afflict themfelves, and fpend their whole life in hard labour: and yet they do not value themfelves upon that, nor leffen other people's credit, that by fo doing they may raife their own; but by their ftooping to fuch fervile employments, they are fo far from being defpifed, that they are fo much the more efteemed by the whole nation.

Of these there are two sorts: Some live unmarried and chaste, and abstain from eating any sort of flesh; and thus weaning themselves from all the pleasures of the present life, which they account hurtful, they pursue even by the hardest and painfullest methods possible, that blessedness which they hope for hereafter; and the nearer they approach to it, they are the more chearful and earnest in their endeavours after it. Another sort of them is less willing to put themselves to much toil, and so they prefer a married state to a single one; and as they do not deny themselves the pleasure of it, so they think the begetting of children is a debt which they owe to human nature, and to their country; nor do they avoid any pleasure that does not hinder labour; and therefore they eat flesh so much the more willingly, because they find themselves so much the more able for work by it: the Utopians look upon these as the wiser sect, but they esteem the others as the holier. They would indeed laugh at any man, that upon the principles of reason, would prefer an unmarried state to a married, or a life of labour to an easy life: but they reverence and admire such as do it upon a motive of religion. There is nothing in which they are more cautious, than in giving their opinion positively concerning any sort of religion. The men that lead those severe lives, are called in the language of their country Brutheskas, which answers to those we call religious orders.

be either killed or taken; and in cafe of the like misfortune to him, the third comes in his place; and thus they provide againſt ill events, that ſuch accidents as may befal their generals, may not endanger their armies. When they draw out troops of their own people, they take ſuch out of every city as freely offer themſelves, for none are forced to go againſt their wills, ſince they think that if any man is preſſed that wants courage, he will not only act faintly, but by his cowardice he will diſhearten others. But if any invaſion is made of their country, they make uſe of ſuch men, if they have good bodies, tho' they are not brave; and either put them aboard their ſhips, or place them on the walls of their towns, that being ſo poſted, they may not find occaſions of flying away; and thus either ſhame, the heat of action, or the impoſſibility of flying, bears down their cowardice; and ſo they make often a virtue of neceſſity, and behave themſelves well, becauſe nothing elſe is left them. But as they force no man to go into any foreign war againſt his will, ſo they do not hinder ſuch women as are willing to go along with their huſbands: On the contrary, they encourage and praiſe them much for doing it; they ſtand often next their huſbands in the front of the army. They alſo place thoſe that are related together, and parents, and children, kindred, and thoſe that are mutually allied, near one another; that thoſe whom nature has inſpired with the greateſt zeal of aſſiſting one another, may be the nearest and readiest to do it; and it is matter of great reproach, if husband or wife survive one another, or if a child survives his parent, and therefore when they come to be engaged in action, they continue to fight to the last man, if their enemies stand before them: And as they use all prudent methods to avoid the endangering their own men; and if it is possible, let all the action and danger fall upon the troops that they hire; so if it comes to that, that they must engage, they charge then with as much courage, as they avoided it before with prudence: nor is it a fierce charge at first, but it increases by degrees; and as they continue in action, they grow more obstinate, and press harder upon the enemy, insomuch that they will much sooner die than give ground; for the certainty in which they are, that their children will be well looked after, when they are dead, frees them from all anxiety concerning them, which does often master men of great courage; and thus they are animated by a noble and invincible resolution. Their skill in military matters increases their courage; and the good opinions which are infused in them during their education, according to the laws of the country, and their learning, add more vigour to their minds: for as they do not undervalue life to the degree of throwing it away too prodigally; so they are not so indecently fond of it, that when they see they must sacrifice it honourably, they will preserve it by base and unbecoming methods.

In the greatest heat of action, the bravest of their youth, that have jointly devoted themselves for that piece of service, single out the general of their enemies, and set on him either openly, or lay an ambuscade for him: If any of them are spent and wearied in the attempt, others come in their stead, so that they never give over pursuing him, either by close weapons, when they can get near him, or those that wound at a distance, when others get in between: thus they seldom fail to kill or take him at last, if he does not secure himself by flight. When they gain the day in any battle, they kill as few as possibly they can; and are much more set on taking many prisoners, than on killing those that fly before them: nor do they ever let their men so loose in the pursuit of their enemies, that they do not retain an entire body still in order; so that if they have been forced to engage the last of their battalions, before they could gain the day, they will rather let their enemies all escape than pursue them, when their own army is in disorder; remembring well what has often fallen out to themselves; that when the main body of their army has been quite defeated and broken, so that their enemies reckoning the victory was sure and in their hands, have let themselves loose into an irregular pursuit, a few of them that lay for a reserve, waiting a fit opportunity, have fallen on them while they were in this chace, straggling in disorder, apprehensive of no danger, but counting the day their own; and have turned the whole action, and so wresting out of their hands a victory that seemed certain and undoubted, the vanquished have of a sudden become victorious.

It is hard to tell whether they are more dexterous in laying or avoiding ambushes: they sometimes seem to fly when it is far from their thoughts; and when they intend to give ground, they do it so, that it is very hard to find out their design. If they see they are ill posted, or are like to be overpowered by numbers, then they either march off in the night with great silence, or by some stratagem they delude their enemies: if they retire in the day time, they do it in such order, that it is no less dangerous to fall upon them in a retreat, than in a march. They fortify their camps well, with a deep and large trench; and throw up the earth that is dug out of it for a wall; nor do they employ only their slaves in this, but the whole army works at it, except those that are then upon the guard; so that when so many hands are at work, a great line and a strong fortification is finished in so short a time, that it is scarce credible. Their armour is very strong for defence, and yet is not so heavy as to make them uneasy in their marches; they can even swim with it. All that are trained up to war, practise swimming much: Both horse and foot make great use of arrows, and are very expert at it: they have no swords, but fight with a poll ax that is both sharp and heavy, by which they thrust or strike down an enemy.; they are very good at finding out warlike machines, and difguife them fo well, that the enemy does not perceive them, till he feels the ufe of them; fo that he cannot prepare fuch a defence againft them, by which they might be made ridiculous, as well as ufelefs; the chief confideration had in the making of them, is, that they may be eafily carried and managed.

If they agree to a truce, they obferve it fo religioufly, that no provocations will make them break it. They never lay their enemies country wafte, nor burn their corn, and even in their marches they take all poffible care, that neither horfe nor foot may tread it down, for they do not know but that they may have ufe for it themfelves. They hurt no man that they find difarmed, unlefs he is a fpy. When a town is furrendered to them, they take it into their protection: and when they carry a place by ftorm, they never plunder it, but put thofe only to the fword that oppofed the rendring it up, and make the reft of the garrifon flaves, but for the other inhabitants, they do them no hurt; and if any of them had advifed a furrender of it, they give them good rewards out of the eftates of thofe that they condemn, and diftribute the reft among their auxiliary troops, but they themfelves take no fhare of the fpoil.

When a war is ended, they do not oblige their friends to reimburfe them of their expence in it; but they take that from the conquered, either in money, which they keep for the next occasion, or in lands, out of which a constant revenue is to be paid them; by many increases, the revenue which they draw out from several countries on such occasions, is now risen to above 700,000 ducats a year. They send some of their own people to receive these revenues, who have orders to live magnificently, and like princes, and so they consume much of it upon the place; and either bring over the rest to Utopia, or lend it to that nation in which it lies. This they most commonly do, unless some great occasion, which falls out but very seldom, should oblige them to call for it all. It is out of these lands that they assign those rewards to such as they encourage to adventure on desperate attempts, which was mentioned formerly. If any prince that engages in war with them, is making preparations for invading their country, they prevent him, and make his country the seat of the war; for they do not willingly suffer any war to break in upon their island; and if that should happen, they would only defend themselves by their own people; but would not at all call for auxiliary troops to their assistance.

Of the Religions of the UTOPIANS.

THERE are several sorts of religions, not only in different parts of the island, but even in every town; some worshipping the sun, others the moon, or one of the planets: some worship such men as have been eminent in former times for virtue, or glory, not only as ordinary deities, but as the supreme God: yet the greater and wiser sort of them worship none of these, but adore one eternal, invisible, infinite, and incomprehensible Deity; as a being that is far above all our apprehensions, that is spread over the whole universe, not by its bulk, but by its power and virtue; him they call the *Father of all*, and acknowledge that the beginnings, the increase, the progress, the vicissitudes, and the end of all things come only from him; nor do they offer divine honours to any but to him alone. And indeed, tho' they differ concerning other things, yet all agree in this; that they think there is one supreme Being that made and governs the world, whom they call in the language of their country, Mithras. They differ in this, that one thinks the God whom he worships is this supreme Being, and another thinks that his idol is that God; but they all agree in one principle, that whatever is this supreme Being, is also that great essence, to whose glory and majesty all honours are ascribed by the consent of all nations.

By degrees, they all fall off from the various superstitions that are among them, and grow up to that one religion that is most in request, and is much the best; and there is no doubt to be made, but that all the others had vanished long ago, if it had not happened that some unlucky accidents, falling on those who were advising the change of those superstitious ways of worship; these have been ascribed not to chance, but to somewhat from Heaven; and so have raised in them a fear, that the God, whose worship was like to be abandoned, has interposed and revenged himself on those that designed it.

After they had heard from us, an account of the doctrine, the course of life, and the miracles of Christ, and of the wonderful constancy of so many martyrs, whose blood that was so willingly offered up by them, was the chief occasion of spreading their religion over a vast number of nations; it is not to be imagined how inclined they were to receive it. I shall not determine whether this proceeded from any secret inspiration of God, or whether it was because it seemed so favourable to that community of goods, which is an opinion so particular, as well as so dear to them; since they perceived that Christ and his followers lived by that rule; and that it was still kept up in some communities among the sincerest sort of Christians. From which soever of these motives it might be, true it is, that many of them came over to our religion, and were initia-

Their priests are men of eminent piety, and therefore they are but few, for there are only thirteen in every town, one for every temple in it; but when they go to war, seven of these go out with their forces, and seven others are chosen to supply their room in their absence; but these enter again upon their employment when they return; and those who served in their absence, attend upon the high-priest, till vacancies fall by death; for there is one that is set over all the rest. They are chosen by the people as the other magistrates are, by suffrages given in secret, for preventing of factions: and when they are chosen, they are consecrated by the college of priests. The care of all sacred things, and the worship of God, and an inspection into the manners of the people, is committed to them. It is a reproach to a man to be sent for by any of them, or to be even spoke to in secret by them, for that always gives some suspicions: all that is incumbent on them, is only to exhort and admonish people; for the power of correcting and punishing ill men, belongs wholly to the prince, and to the other magistrates: the severest thing that the priest does, is the excluding of men that are desperately wicked from joining in their worship: there's not any sort of punishment that is more dreaded by them than this, for as it loads them with infamy, so it fills them with secret horrors, such is their reverence to their religion; nor will their bodies be long exempted from their share of trouble; for if they do not very quickly satisfy the priests of the truth of their repentance, they are seized on by the senate, and punished for their impiety. The breeding of the youth belongs to the priests, yet they do not take so much care of instructing them in letters, as of forming their minds and manners aright; and they use all possible methods to infuse very early in the tender and flexible minds of children, such opinions as are both good in themselves, and will be useful to their country: for when deep impressions of these things are made at that age, they follow men through the whole course of their lives, and conduce much for the preserving the peace of the government, which suffers by nothing more than by vices that rise out of ill opinions. The wives of their priests are the most extraordinary women of the whole country; sometimes the women themselves are made priests, tho' that falls out but seldom, nor are any but antient widows chosen into that order.

None of the magistrates have greater honour paid them, than is paid the priests; and if they should happen to commit any crime, they would not be questioned for it: their punishment is left to God, and to their own consciences: for they do not think it lawful to lay hands on any man, how wicked soever he is, that has been in a peculiar manner dedicated to God; nor do they find any great inconvenience in this, both because they have so few priests, and because these are chosen with much caution, so that it must be a very unusual thing to find one who was merely out of regard to his virtue, and for his being esteemed a singularly good man, raised up to so great a dignity, degenerate into such corruption and vice: and if such a thing should fall out, for man is a changeable creature; yet there being a few priests, and these having no authority, but that which rises out of the respect that is paid them, nothing that is of great consequence to the public, can come from the indemnity that the priests enjoy.

They have indeed very few of them, lest greater numbers sharing in the same honour, might make the dignity of that order which they esteem so highly, to sink in its reputation: they also think it is hard to find out many that are of such a pitch of goodness, as to be equal to that dignity for which they judge that ordinary virtues do not qualify a man sufficiently: nor are the priests in greater veneration among them, than they are among their neighbouring nations, as you may imagine by that which I think gives occasion for it.

When the Utopians engage in a battle, the priests that accompany them to the war, kneel down during the action, in a place not far from the field, apparelled in their sacred vestments: and lifting up their hands to heaven, they pray, first for peace, and then for victory to their own side, and particularly that it may be gained without the effusion of much blood on either side; and when the victory turns to their side, they run in among their own men to restrain their fury; and if any of their enemies fee them, or call to them, they are preserved by that means: and such as can come so near them as to touch their garments, have not only their lives, but their fortunes secured to them: it is upon this account that all the nations round about consider them so much, and pay them so great reverence, that they have been often no less able to preserve their own people from the fury of their enemies, than to save their enemies from their rage: for it has sometimes fallen out, that when their armies have been in disorder, and forced to fly, so that their enemies were running upon the slaughter and spoil, the priests by interposing, have stop'd the shedding of more blood, and have separated them from one another; so that by their mediation, a peace has been concluded on very reasonable terms; nor is there any nation about them so fierce, cruel, or barbarous, as not to look upon their persons as sacred and inviolable.

The first and the last day of the month, and of the year, is a festival: they measure their months by the course of the moon; and their years by the course of the sun: the first days are called in their language the Cynemernes, and the last the Trapemernes, which answers in our language to the festival that begins, or ends the season.

They have magnificent temples, that are not only nobly built, but are likewise of great reception: which is necessary, since they have so few of them: they are a little dark within, which flows not from any error in their architecture, but is done on defign; for their priefts think that too much light diffipates the thoughts, and that a more moderate degree of it, both recollects the mind, and raifes devotion. Tho' there are many different forms of religion among them, yet all thefe, how various foever, agree in the main point, which is the worfhipping the divine effence; and therefore there is nothing to be feen or heard in their temples, in which the feveral perfuafions among them may not agree; for every fect performs thofe rites that are peculiar to it, in their private houfes, nor is their any thing in the public worfhip, that contradicts the particular ways of thofe different fects. There are no images for God in their temples, fo that every one may reprefent him to his thoughts, according to the way of his religion; nor do they call this one God by any other name, but that of Mithras, which is the common name by which they all exprefs the divine effence, whatfoever otherwife they think it to be; nor are there any prayers among them, but fuch as every one of them may ufe without prejudice to his own opinion.

They meet in their temples on the evening of the feftival that concludes a feafon: and not having yet broke their faft, they thank God for their good fuccefs during that year or month, which is then at an end: and the next day, being that which begins the new feafon, they meet early in their temples, to pray for the happy progress of all their affairs during that period, upon which they then enter. In the festival which concludes the period, before they go to the temple, both wives and children fall on their knees before their husbands or parents, and confess every thing in which they have either erred or failed in their duty, and beg pardon for it: thus all little discontents in families are removed, that so they may offer up their devotions with a pure and serene mind; for they hold it a great impiety to enter upon them with disturbed thoughts; or when they are conscious to themselves that they bear hatred or anger in their hearts to any person; and think that they should become liable to severe punishments, if they presumed to offer sacrifices without cleansing their hearts, and reconciling all their differences. In the temples, the two sexes are separated, the men go to the right hand, and the women to the left; and the males and females do all place themselves before the head, and master or mistress of that family to which they belong; so that those who have the government of them at home, may see their deportment in public. And they intermingle them so, that the younger and the older may be set by one another; for if the younger sort were all set together, they would perhaps trifle away that time too much, in which they ought to beget in themselves a most religious dread of the supream being, which is the greatest, and almost the only incitement to virtue.

They offer up no living creature in sacrifice, nor do

they think it suitable to the divine being, from whose bounty it is that these creatures have derived their lives, to take pleasure in their death, or the offering up their blood. They burn incense, and other sweet odours, and have a great number of wax lights during their worship; not out of any imagination that such oblations can add any thing to the divine nature, for even prayers do not that; but as it is a harmless and pure way of worshipping God, so they think those sweet favours and lights, together with some other ceremonies, do, by a secret and unaccountable virtue, elevate men's souls, and inflame them with more force and chearfulness during the divine worship.

The people appear all in the temples in white garments; but the priest's vestments are parti-coloured; both the work and colours are wonderful: they are made of no rich materials, for they are neither embroidered, nor set with precious stones, but are composed of the plumes of several birds, laid together with so much art, and so neatly, that the true value of them is far beyond the costliest materials. They say, that in the ordering and placing those plumes, some dark mysteries are represented, which pass down among their priests in a secret tradition concerning them; and that they are as Hieroglyphics, putting them in mind of the blessings that they have received from God, and of their duties, both to him and to their neighbours. As soon as the priest appears in those ornaments, they all fall postrate on the ground, with so much reverence and so deep a silence, that such as look on, cannot but be struck with it, as if it were the effect of the appearance of a deity. After they have been for some time in this posture, they all stand up, upon a sign given by the priest, and sing some hymns to the honour of God, some musical instruments playing all the while. These are quite of another form than those that are used among us: but, as many of them are much sweeter than ours, so others are not to be compared to those that we have. Yet in one thing they exceed us much, which is, that all their music, both vocal and instrumental, does so imitate and express the passions, and is so fitted to the present occasion, whether the subject-matter of the hymn is chearful, or made to appease, or trouble, doleful, or angry; that the music makes an impression of that which is represented, by which it enters deep into the hearers, and does very much affect and kindle them. When this is done, both priests and people offer up very solemn prayers to God in a set form of words; and these are so composed, that whatsoever is pronounced by the whole assembly, may be likewise applied by every man in particular to his own condition; in these they acknowledge God to be the author and governor of the world, and the fountain of all the good that they receive; for which they offer up their thanksgivings to him; and in particular, they bless him for his goodness in ordering it so, that they are born under a government that is the happiest in the world, and are of a religion that they hope is the truest of all others: but if they are mistaken, and if there is either a better government, or a religion more acceptable to God, they implore his goodness to let them know it, vowing that they resolve to follow him whithersoever he leads them: but if their government is the best, and their religion the truest, then they pray that he may fortify them in it, and bring all the world, both to the same rules of life, and to the same opinions concerning himself; unless, according to the unsearchableness of his mind, he is pleased with a variety of religions. Then they pray that God may give them an easy passage at last to himself; not presuming to set limits to him, how early or late it should be; but if it may be wished for, without derogating from his supream authority, they desire rather to be quickly delivered, and to go to God, tho' by the terriblest sort of death, than to be detained long from seeing him, in the most prosperous course of life possible. When this prayer is ended, they all fall down again upon the ground, and after a little while they rise up, and go home to dinner; and spend the rest of the day in diversion or military exercises.

Thus have I described to you, as particularly as I could, the constitution of that common-wealth, which I do not only think to be the best in the world, but to be indeed the only common-wealth that truly deserves that name In all other places, it is visible, that whereas people talk of a common-wealth, every man only seeks his own wealth; but there, where no man has any property, all men do zealously pursue the good of the public: and indeed, it is no wonder to see men act so differently, for in other common-wealths, every man knows, that unless he provides for himself, how flourishing soever the common-wealth may be, he must die of hunger; so that he sees the necessity of preferring his own concerns to the public; but in Utopia, where every man has a right to every thing, they do all know, that if care is taken to keep the public stores full, no private man can want any thing; for among them there is no unequal distribution, so that no man is poor, nor in any necessity; and tho' no man has any thing, yet they are all rich; for what can make a man so rich, as to lead a serene and chearful life, free from anxieties; neither apprehending want himself, nor vexed with the endless complaints of his wife? He is not afraid of the misery of his children, nor is he contriving how to raise a portion for his daughters, but is secure in this, that both he and his wife, his children and grandchildren, to as many generations as he can fancy, will all live, both plentifully and happily, since among them there is no less care taken of those who were once engaged in labour, but grow afterwards unable to follow it, than there is elsewhere for these that continue still at it. I would gladly hear any man compare the justice that is among them, with that which is among all other nations; among whom, may I perish, if I see any thing that looks either like justice, or equity; for what justice is there in this, that a nobleman, a goldsmith, or a banquer, or any other man, that either does nothing at all, or at best is employed in things that are of no use to the public, should live in great luxury, and splendor, upon that which is so ill acquired; and a mean man, a carter, a smith, or a ploughman, that works harder, even than the beasts themselves, and is employed in labours that are so necessary, that no commonwealth could hold out an year to an end without them, can yet be able to earn so poor a livelihood out of it, and must lead so miserable a life in it, that the beasts condition is much better than theirs? For as the beasts do not work so constantly, so they feed almost as well, and more pleasantly; and have no anxiety about that which is to come, whereas these men are depressed by a barren and fruitless employment, and are tormented with the apprehensions of want in their old age; since that which they get by their daily labour, does but maintain them at present, and is consumed as fast as it comes in; so that there is no overplus left them which they can lay up for old age.

Is not that government both unjust and ungrateful, that is so prodigal of its favours, to those that are called gentlemen, or goldsmiths, or such others that are idle, or live either by flattery, or by contriving the arts of vain pleasure; and on the other hand, takes no care of those of a meaner sort, such as ploughmen, soldiers, and smiths, without whom it could not subsist: but after the public has been served by them, and that they come to be oppressed with age, sickness, and want, all their labours and the good that they have done is forgotten; and all the recompense given them, is, that they are left to die in great misery: and the richer sort are often endeavouring to bring the hire of labourers lower, not only by their fraudulent practices, but by the laws which they procure to be made to that effect: so that tho' it is a thing most unjust in itself, to give such small rewards to those who deserve so well of the public, yet they have given these hardships the name and colour of justice, by procuring laws to be made for regulating it.

Therefore I must say, that as I hope for mercy, I can have no other notion of all the other governments that I see or know, than that they are a conspiracy of the richer sort, who on pretence of managing the public, do only pursue their private ends, and devise all the ways and arts that they can find out; first, that they may, without danger, preserve all that they have so ill acquired, and then, that they may engage the poorer sort to toil and labour for them, at as low rates as is possible, and oppress them as much as they please: and if they can but prevail to get these contrivances established, by the show of public authority, which is considered as the representative of the whole people, then they are accounted laws: and yet thefe wicked men after they have by a moſt inſatiable covetouſneſs, divided that among themſelves, with which all the reſt might have been well ſupplied, are far from that happineſs, that is enjoyed among the Utopians: for the uſe as well as the deſire of money being extinguiſhed, there is much anxiety and great occaſions of miſchief cut off with it: and who does not ſee that frauds, thefts, robberies, quarrels, tumults, contentions, ſeditions, murders, treacheries, and witchcrafts, that are indeed rather puniſhed than reſtrained by the ſeverities of law, would all fall off, if money were not any more valued by the world? Men's fears, ſolicitudes, cares, labours, and watchings, would all periſh in the ſame moment, that the value of money did ſink: even poverty itſelf, for the relief of which money ſeems moſt neceſſary, would fall, if there were no money in the world. And in order to the apprehending this aright, take one inſtance.

Conſider any year that has been ſo unfruitful, that many thouſands have died of hunger; and yet if at the end of that year a ſurvey were made of the granaries of all the rich men that have hoarded up the corn, it would be found that there was enough among them, to have prevented all that conſumption of men that periſhed in that miſery: and that if it had been diſtributed among them, none would have felt the terrible effects of that ſcarcity; ſo eaſy a thing would it be to ſupply all the neceſſities of life, if that bleſſed thing called money, that is pretended to be invented for procuring it, were not really the only thing that obstructed it.

I do not doubt but rich men are sensible of this, and that they know well how much a greater happiness it were to want nothing that were necessary, than to abound in many superfluities; and to be rescued out of so much misery, than to abound with so much wealth: and I cannot think but the sense of every man's interest, and the authority of Christ's commands, who as he was infinitely wise, and so knew what was best, so was no less good in discovering it to us, would have drawn all the world over to the laws of the Utopians, if pride, that plague of human nature, that is the source of so much misery, did not hinder it; which does not measure happiness so much by its own conveniences, as by the miseries of others; and would not be satisfied with being thought a goddess, if none were left that were miserable, over whom she might insult; and thinks its own happiness shines the brighter, by comparing it with the misfortunes of other persons; that so by displaying its own wealth, they may feel their poverty the more sensibly. This is that infernal serpent that creeps into the breasts of mortals, and possesses them too much to be easily drawn out: and therefore I am glad that the Utopians have fallen upon this form of government, in which I wish that all the world could be so wise as to imitate them: for they have indeed laid down such a scheme and foundation of policy, that as men live happy under it, so it is like to be of great continuance: for they having rooted out of the minds of their people, all the seeds, both of ambition and faction, there is no danger of any commotions at home: which alone has been the ruin of many states, that seemed otherwise to be well secured; but as long as they live in peace at home, and are governed by such good laws, the envy of all their neighbouring princes, who have often attempted their ruin, but in vain, will never be able to put their state into any commotion or disorder.

When Raphael had thus made an end of speaking, tho' many things occurred to me, both concerning the manners and laws of that people, that seemed very absurd, as well in their way of making war, as in their notions of religion, and divine matters; together with several other particulars, but chiefly that which seemed the foundation of all the rest, their living in common, without any use of money, by which all nobility, magnificence, splendour and majesty; which, according to the common opinion, are the true ornaments of a nation, would be quite taken away; yet since I perceived that Raphael was weary, and I was not sure whether he could easily bear contradiction in these matters, remembring that he had taken notice of some, who seemed to think that they were bound in honour for supporting the credit of their own wisdom, to find out some matter of censure in all other men's inventions, besides their own; therefore, I only commended their constitution, and the account he had given of it in general; and so taking him by the hand, I carried him to supper, and told him I would find out some other time for examining that matter more particularly, and for discoursing more copiously concerning it; for which I wish I may find a good opportunity. In the mean while, tho' I cannot perfectly agree to every thing that was related by Raphael, yet there are many things in the commonwealth of Utopia, that I rather wish than hope to see followed in our governments; tho' it must be confessed, that he is both a very learned man, and has had a great practice in the world.

F I N I S.

www.ingramcontent.com/pod-product-compliance
Lightning Source LLC
Chambersburg PA
CBHW031618170426
43195CB00037B/850